I Said My Piece with Peace

Inside USAID's Final Days

A Testament of Leadership When Everything Falls Apart

Keisha L. Effiom

Unmuted Press

Published by Unmuted Press

ISBN: 979-4-310975-3-4

First Edition, 2025

Printed in the United States of America

www.keishaeffiom.com
Author@keishaeffiom.com

Dedication

To the people I was honored to lead in Rwanda and Burundi.

To my mother and my sister, whose strength runs through me.

To my sistah friends, my ride and thrives.

And to my husband Vincent, my son Vinnie, and my daughter Zoe,

my anchor in every storm.

Preface: The Swearing-In

"If not you then who?"

I am a servant leader, full stop. I thrive on serving others. It is rooted in my bones. That's how I got here.

So what makes up the DNA of me? My foundation is love. It's that simple and that complicated. But if love is my foundation, music is my oxygen. I carry my father's love and music in my veins, and my mother's unshakeable strength in my spirit. My father sang all the time, in the car, in the kitchen, for no reason at all. I do the same. My daughter does too. It's not a hobby; it's hereditary. It's the thing we reach for when words aren't enough. When I am weary, I sing. When I am grieving, I sing. When I need to remember who I am before the titles and the pressures and the politics, I sing. Music has lifted me out of moments that might have otherwise broken me. It is woven into my fabric, passed down like eye color or stubbornness, and I will pass it to whatever comes after me. I am grounded in my faith which allows me to lead with humility. I am unapologetic about who I am, and that confidence was nurtured by my sister's love and my brother's protective spirit. My husband sees something in me that even I sometimes miss: "She is one of the most considerate persons I have ever met. She knows and is aware of double standards in the world. However, she will ask you to consider how you would feel if the reverse were the case." That perspective, that ability to flip the script and demand empathy, would become central to everything I did as a leader.

My love for Africa began long before I ever imagined serving there. At the Academic Enrichment Center, now Bridges Academy, where I spent ten years from kindergarten through eighth grade, we learned to stand tall and proud of the fact that we are descendants of Africans. From book reports about Ghana to our African dance troupe performing on the stage of the Apollo, these were the unforgettable building blocks that built my confidence and pride in my cultural heritage.

It was Ms. Campbell, our school principal, who loved each of us as her own children, believing in all our individual talents, ensuring our light was always bright and wings never clipped. She told us to always reach for the stars, believe in ourselves, "because nothing is impossible". At Howard University, the melting pot of different cultures that further strengthened my connection to the continent, my communications professors started each class saying, "We must reside in the upper echelons of excellence." This was another fundamental building block in reaching for the stars and achieving my goals.

Through it all, my sistah friends, my crew, the ones who aren't blood but my family, allowed me to be vulnerable without judgment, cheering me on when I wasn't looking. When my crown was slightly crooked, they adjusted it, reaching out their hands to build me up, never tearing me down. They truly live and breathe the saying that "empowered women, empower women."

And my anchor, Jay, the honey to my tea, who pushes me to reach for the stars and beyond. My children, Vinnie and Zoe, braver than they believe, stronger than they seem, smarter than they think, and loved more than they know. My mother, a beautiful soul, soft around the edges and tempered with a spine of steel, who taught me the most important thing in life: your faith comes first, everything else will follow.

July 18th, 2024. The date had been circled on my calendar for months, but it felt like it had been written in my heart for years.

One of the greatest accomplishments of my professional career, I was sworn in by Samantha Power, former United States Agency for International Development (USAID) Administrator, as the Mission Director for Rwanda and Burundi. I had been preparing for this moment, dreamt about this moment, and now the day was finally here. Family and friends came to the Nation's Capital to witness this milestone in my career. It was time.

I prepared for that day like it was my wedding. Make-up, check. Outfit, check. Reception venue, check. Food, check. Cake, check. Most importantly, I was ready. I spent seven months preparing my acceptance speech because I didn't want to miss thanking anyone.

Everyone in my life played a significant role in this accomplishment.

Of particular significance: I was one of only eight African American women working for USAID in the esteemed position of Mission Director, out of 60-90 around the world. To understand what that means, consider this: the Mission Director is the highest-ranking USAID official in any country, the face of American development investment, sitting on the U.S. Ambassador's Country Team. I managed a $100 million+ portfolio across two nations, Rwanda and Burundi, with more than 100 staff under my leadership. Over my career, I had overseen more than $2 billion in development funding. This wasn't a desk job. This was shaping U.S. foreign assistance on the ground.

The Ronald Reagan Building was electric that day. Standing room only. Hundreds packed into the space, with over 600 more watching online, people who had traveled from across the country, colleagues who had served beside me on three continents, friends who had known me since before I knew what a Mission Director even was. My childhood principal was there. And everywhere I looked: purple. Shades of purple filling the room like a coronation, because the people who loved me knew it was my favorite color. They had coordinated without telling me. I stood there taking it all in, and one thought kept circling: This cannot be real. This cannot be my life.

So, when it was time to take my oath and deliver my speech, I stood tall. At 5'4", I felt like I was seven feet. I felt my feet planted and rooted on the ground where so many had fought and sacrificed to get me here. Head held high, I looked across the room and saw the smiles, the tears, the sense of pride in every single person there.

Hand raised. Heart pounding. The weight of possibility settling on my shoulders like a mantle I'd been preparing to wear my entire career.

"I, Keisha Lanai Effiom, affirm that I will well and faithfully discharge the duties of the office to which I am about to enter."

The words carried the weight of everything that had brought me to this moment. My mother's life force that had taught me to be strong. My father's pearls of wisdom about navigating life's challenges with confidence and grace. The colleagues who'd watched me stand up when it was the right thing to do, like the time I fought for our local employees over that parking policy, despite being cautioned not to get involved. Because dignity matters. Because people matter.

Take care of people and they will take care of you. The motto I'd lived by in every role, every mission, every challenging situation. Ambassador Sharon Cromer had seen it clearly: my "one thing" was people. Not programs, not policies, not career advancement - people. The contractor I'd rushed to introduce around the room in Tanzania because nobody should feel alone in a new place. The small businesses I'd championed as a Contracting Officer, leading co-creation workshops across West Africa, finding ways to get to "Yes" when others saw only restrictions.

They knew about my legendary collection of eyeglasses and my tendency to curate farewell parties like wedding ceremonies with juice bars and printed programs, because celebrating people mattered. They knew about my surprising introversion that left me exhausted after days of engaging everyone, sending me home to curl up with Golden Girls reruns to recharge.

They knew the whole person standing before them taking this oath. And they were here, physically and virtually, because they believed in what that person could accomplish.

As I spoke those words in my acceptance speech, looking out at faces filled with love and pride, I shared what was in my heart:

"Today I pledge to my team my unwavering commitment to lead with integrity, empathy, and dedication. I firmly believe that leadership is not about authority or power, but rather about service and empowerment. My primary goal will be to continue to foster an inclusive and collaborative environment where each and every one of you feels valued, heard, and empowered to contribute your best, and to start good trouble, as the late John Lewis would say, when necessary."

I felt the profound responsibility and extraordinary opportunity converging as I declared to everyone listening:

"THE TIME IS NOW, MY TIME IS NOW, OUR TIME IS NOW!"

I knew that in that moment, the time was now. MY TIME was now, and I was hopeful and proud.

I had plans...big, bold, beautiful plans. Partnerships that would last generations. Trusted alliances that would transform communities. Programs that would touch lives in ways we hadn't even imagined yet. I was pumped. Ready. This was our time.

Standing there, surrounded by people who'd supported my journey, I felt pure, undiluted possibility. I was a servant leader who'd been given the platform to serve at the highest level. Everything I'd learned about taking care of people, everything my parents had taught me about strength and grace, everything my colleagues had witnessed about my commitment to doing right even when it was difficult, all of it was about to be put to the ultimate test.

I had no idea how brutally, how completely, how devastatingly that test would come.

But in that moment, hand just lowered from the oath, surrounded by love and possibility and the weight of history, I was ready for anything.

Well, at least I thought I was ready for anything.

Part I: The Sacred Work We Called Home

Chapter 1: The Calling vs. The Job

"USAID wasn't just my workplace, it was my mission field, my platform for impact, my home."

Some people have jobs. I was blessed with something rarer: a calling that aligned with my soul.

For eighteen years, USAID wasn't just my workplace, it was my mission field, my platform for impact, my home. I didn't just work there; I belonged there. Every program launched, every partnership forged, every life touched, it all mattered. It all meant something.

When I was sworn in as Mission Director for Rwanda and Burundi, most people outside the foreign service world didn't understand what that meant. Let me break it down: A Mission Director is the highest-ranking USAID official in a country, essentially the CEO of American development assistance for an entire nation, or in my case, two nations.

While the Ambassador is the President's representative and leads the entire U.S. presence in a country, I led our development portfolio, over $200 million in annual programs. I managed teams of hundreds, American and local staff. I negotiated directly with presidents and ministers on development partnerships. When disease outbreaks threatened communities, when farmers needed agricultural support, when children needed nutrition programs, those decisions came to my desk.

In the country team meetings at the Embassy, I sat at the table with the Ambassador, the Deputy Chief of Mission, the Department of Defense Attaché, and other agency heads, representing USAID's voice in shaping American foreign policy. I was America's face of development partnership, not dominance, not charity, but partnership.

It's a position that typically takes decades to achieve. The weight of it, the responsibility of stewarding taxpayer dollars while serving vulnerable communities, requires a particular kind of leadership.

And I was one of only eight African American women in the world holding this position.

For readers who only know Rwanda from Hotel Rwanda, let me offer a fuller picture. Yes, Rwanda is a country still healing from the 1994 Genocide against the Tutsis. But it is so much richer and deeper than that singular tragedy.

Rwanda is a force to be reckoned with. Complicated, strong, and healing. This is not a nation that can be bullied. The people have been through things you wouldn't wish on your worst enemy, but if you can find space in their battle-tested hearts, if you can earn their trust, you are loved. Fiercely, loyally loved. But break that trust? You never get it back.

They call it the Land of a Thousand Hills, and it has the absolute best weather anyone could ask for. Tourism is rising, with gorilla trekking drawing visitors from around the world. The Basketball Africa League and Giants of Africa have put Rwanda on the global sports map. This is a country on the rise, determined to write its own future.

In Rwanda, USAID operated across four technical areas: health, education, democracy and governance, and economic growth. We weren't just present; we were partners in the country's transformation.

Burundi is different but equally remarkable. Shaped like a heart, it is known as the Heart of Africa. It is also the world's poorest country, with the highest childhood stunting rate on earth. The people are magnificent, warm, and kind, but the nation suffers from real democracy and governance issues. Burundi was an office, not a full mission, because we worked mainly in health and humanitarian assistance, the most urgent needs for the most vulnerable people.

When USAID was dismantled, host governments around the world didn't publicly mourn. My hunch is they felt the destruction deeply but would never admit it. And why should they? Africa doesn't want to be seen as needing handouts. Africa wants to be seen for what it is: a powerful force, a continent no other continent could survive without, including the United States. This wasn't charity. This was partnership. And when America walked away, Africa kept standing, because that's what Africa does.

But my people, my teams in Rwanda and Burundi, they couldn't hide what this did to them. These were the people who gave me hugs on a random Tuesday just because. The ones who invited me to their weddings, into their homes, to share meals with their families. We laughed together. We cried together. We built something together.

And then it was taken. Some of my colleagues couldn't get loans from the bank because of how we were labeled. People who had dedicated their lives to public service suddenly couldn't finance a car or a home. That was the betrayal. Not just the closure of an agency, but the destruction of people's dignity, their reputations, their futures.

There's a difference between working for an organization and being called to serve its mission. When you have a job, you clock in, perform your duties, and go home. When you have a calling, the work follows you everywhere. It shapes how you see the world, how you measure success, how you define your own worth.

I could have worked anywhere. With my legal background and contracting expertise, corporate opportunities knocked regularly. Better hours, higher pay, fewer complications. But every time I considered those offers, something inside me resisted. This wasn't about career advancement; this was about purpose.

The Work That Chose Me

Development work is unique. We measure our success by the day the world no longer needs us. A world free from poverty, corruption, disease, that's the dream. That's the goal we're working ourselves out of. How many professions can say their ultimate objective is to make themselves obsolete?

That paradox drew me in from day one. The audacity of it. The hope embedded in believing that change was possible, that systems could be strengthened, that lives could be transformed through partnership and persistent effort.

But here's what I learned early: development isn't about programs or policies or perfectly crafted theories of change. It's about people. Real people with real hopes and real challenges who deserve dignity, opportunity, and the chance to shape their own futures.

That's where servant leadership became essential.

What My Mentors Taught Me

The servant leadership philosophy I brought to USAID wasn't born in a vacuum. It was shaped by mentors who understood that development work requires a different kind of leadership, one rooted in grace, expertise, and genuine care for people.

Ambassador Cromer taught me one of my most important lessons: give grace. "Grace for myself and grace for others," she would say. "Grace builds relationships, establishes trust and deepens respect. It makes you an effective leader and diplomat." That lesson became my core leadership philosophy.

Jamala Peyton and Sheila Bumpass taught me the importance of knowing my craft. "Take the time to master it; become an expert, because that is something that is in your control," they advised. When I joined the Foreign Service, their guidance was simple but profound: be a good leader, know your job, and find ways to yes!

Ambassador Alfonso Lenhardt gave me the motto that would define my entire approach: "Take care of your people and they will take care of you." That statement impacted me deeply and influenced my leadership style. I experienced the lasting results of building an environment where people want to be and thrive.

Jonathan Kamin taught me to ask the tough questions and look under the surface. "It helps us to be "real thought leaders," he would say. It gets us to the core of problem-solving and enables us to make significant changes, the type of sustainable change needed in development work.

But perhaps most importantly, I learned that knowing the family members of my team, how many kids a person has, if their mom is sick or if a grandchild was born, is just as important as knowing if our programs are being implemented successfully. It's the human side of the job that I love, being able to recognize if something is wrong by just looking at a person because I have taken the time to get to know them.

Why Servant Leadership Matters in Development

Servant leadership is a philosophy where the leader's primary role is to serve others. Rather than accumulating power or chasing personal success, a servant leader prioritizes the growth, well-being, and empowerment of their team. The leader succeeds when their people succeed.

Traditional leadership says: "I have the answers, follow me."

Servant leadership says: "Let's figure this out together, and I'll make sure everyone has what you need to succeed."

In development work, that distinction is everything. I must admit that over the years, this concept was diluted. Politics can change everything. It dictates the rules and before you know it, you have forgotten what it truly means to be partners. We must remember at the core that we weren't parachuting into communities as saviors with predetermined solutions. We were partners, facilitators, bridges between resources and needs, between possibility and reality.

As I learned from my mentors, leadership is not about authority or power, but rather about service and empowerment. The goal is to foster an inclusive and collaborative environment where each person feels valued, heard, and empowered to contribute their best, and to start "good trouble," as the late John Lewis would say, when necessary.

In my early days as a Contracting Officer, I learned this truth viscerally. I could write the most technically perfect contracts in the world, but if I didn't understand the people implementing them, their constraints, their capabilities, or their cultural context, those contracts would fail. The partnership component would be missing. The relationship then became transactional. For some things that could work, but in development work, where people's lives are at stake and governments' trust is needed, transactional doesn't work.

Partnership does. Success depended on relationships, trust, and genuine care for everyone involved in the process.

That's why I couldn't just process contractors as paperwork. That newcomer in Tanzania I rushed to introduce around the room. He needed to feel welcomed, connected, part of something larger than a transactional relationship. When people feel valued, they perform differently. When they trust you're fighting for their success, they'll move mountains to achieve it.

The Small Business Championship

My approach crystallized during my work championing small businesses. On paper, it was about meeting contracting goals and expanding opportunities for U.S.-based small businesses to compete overseas. In practice, it was about seeing potential where others saw complications.

Small businesses didn't just need contracts, they needed guidance, connections, confidence that someone believed in their ability to deliver. I led co-creation workshops across West Africa, bringing missions together to move beyond traditional business models. Not because it was required, but because it was right.

When USAID Ghana faced a 35% budget cut, conventional wisdom said small business goals would be impossible to meet. But conventional wisdom doesn't account for what happens when you treat people as partners rather than vendors. We didn't just exceed our small business goals, we expanded collaboration in ways that created lasting value.

I was awarded the Small Business Contracting Officer of the year in 2018 and again in 2022. This award wasn't really about contracting expertise. It was recognition that servant leadership works. When you invest in people's success, when you create environments where everyone can thrive, remarkable things happen.

Servant leadership isn't always celebrated. Sometimes it gets you into "good trouble," as the late John Lewis would say.

Early in my time as Acting Deputy Mission Director, I discovered our Foreign Service Nationals, the local staff who are the backbone of every mission, were demoralized by a new parking policy that prioritized limited spaces for American staff. FSNs were frustrated, hurt, and felt abandoned. Tensions were escalating toward a serious crisis.

I was cautioned not to get involved. "Not your lane," they said. "Let someone else handle it."

But servant leadership doesn't recognize lanes when people are hurting. My FSN colleagues weren't just experiencing a parking problem, they were experiencing a dignity problem. They felt valued less than their American counterparts, and that feeling was poisoning the work environment.

So, I facilitated a town hall, creating a safe space for FSNs to express their concerns. I worked with FSN leaders to develop alternative solutions that respected different perspectives and cultures. Through multiple, often contentious meetings, we reached agreement on equitable solutions, including allocating parking on a first-come, first-served basis.

Some thought I was overstepping. I thought I was doing my job. Servant leaders don't get to choose comfortable fights. We fight for what's right, especially when it's inconvenient.

The Art of Getting to "Yes"

Over the years, I became known for finding ways to get to "yes" when others saw only restrictions. Not because I ignored rules or cut corners, but because I understood that behind every policy challenge was a human need worth addressing.

When HIV programs and beneficiaries were threatened, I didn't accept defeat. I found ways to ensure program integrity while protecting at-risk populations. When budget cuts threatened partnerships, I looked for creative solutions that preserved relationships and impact.

This wasn't about being a miracle worker. It was about refusing to let bureaucratic limitations overshadow human possibilities. Servant leadership means you serve the mission, not just the machinery.

What Makes It Sacred

By the time I was sworn in as Mission Director, I understood what made this work sacred. We weren't just implementing programs, we were participating in the ancient human tradition of caring for one another across boundaries of nationality, culture, and circumstance.

Every successful partnership was a small victory against the forces that divide us. Every life improved was proof that people of goodwill can accomplish extraordinary things together. Every system strengthened was an investment in a future where fewer children would grow up without opportunity.

The work was bigger than any individual mission or program. It was about the world we were building for the next generation. That's what made it a calling rather than a career.

Standing in that swearing-in ceremony, surrounded by colleagues who'd become family, I felt the full weight of that calling. This wasn't a promotion, it was a platform to serve at scale, to take everything I'd learned about servant leadership and apply it to some of the most complex development challenges in the world.

I was ready. My teams in Rwanda and Burundi deserved a leader who understood that programs serve people, not the other way around. They deserved someone who would fight for what's right, even when it meant getting into good trouble.

What I didn't know was how soon that fighting would begin, or how much it would cost.

But I knew this: servant leadership wasn't just my approach to the work, it was my approach to life. I am a wife, a mother, a sister, a cousin, a friend, and I was about to discover what that really meant when everything I'd built my career on began to fall apart.

Chapter 2: When Giants Begin to Fall

"Injustice happens every second, everywhere. We read about it, shake our heads, move on. But living it, breathing it, carrying it in your chest like a stone, that hits different. That changes you."

The first whispers came like rumors you hope aren't true. I said to myself, if this happens, we have been here before, we know what to expect. I reassured the team to focus on the present and we will deal with what comes. USAID had weathered political transitions before. New administrations always brought new priorities, new rhetoric, new approaches. We'd adapt, as we always did. The mission was too important, the work too vital, the impact too real for anyone to seriously consider... what? What exactly were they considering?

That was the problem. Nobody knew.

The First Test

Before the shuttering began, I faced my first major test as Mission Director. Just weeks into my new role, Rwanda declared a Marburg outbreak, a deadly hemorrhagic fever that could devastate communities if not contained quickly.

I was in Rwanda when I got the call: nurses at a nearby hospital were dying unexpectedly. No one knew why yet, but the fear was already spreading faster than the virus.

Within days, the embassy went on mandatory telework. Parents were advised to keep their children home. This wasn't happening in some distant province, the outbreak was in Kigali, the capital, where we all lived. Where my family lived.

It was critical not to let panic corrode our thinking.

What followed was development and diplomacy at its finest. We were in lockstep with the Rwandan Ministry of Health, the CDC, WHO, and donor partners. My team became the interlocutor for the State Department, we had the trusted relationships, built over years, that opened doors. We got meetings and access to rooms they couldn't get into without us.

I watched my team mobilize with precision and purpose. No one asked what was in their job description. No one hesitated. This was the work.

The collaboration between the host government and the U.S., the seamless coordination, the mutual respect, the shared urgency, that was the moment I knew: this is why we exist. Not for the paperwork or the politics, but for moments like this, when partnership means the difference between containment and catastrophe.

It was a huge moment of pride. And it was about to be erased.

Standing in those first 90 days as Mission Director, watching USAID's crucial role in protecting public health, I felt the full weight and wonder of what we could accomplish next. We built the relationships, invested in our expertise, nurtured the partnerships, and had a 65-year reputation based on credibility to respond to crises that threatened the most vulnerable populations, and we played a vital role in keeping the borders safe in the homeland.

It was exactly the kind of bold, beautiful impact I'd envisioned when I took my oath.

I had no idea that the very institution capable of this life-saving work was about to be dismantled, illegally.

The Unthinkable Becomes Possible

The recipe for the unthinkable:

- 1 cup of bruised ego
- 1 cup of hate
- 1 cup of ignorance
- 2 cups of mama issues
- 1 cup of zero F's to give

- 1 tablespoon of vindictiveness
- A generous helping of cruelty
- A dash of complete disregard for human consequences
- 1 pound of willful blindness to expertise
- 1 cup of cowardice
- Unlimited amount of "burn it all down"
- Pour until you feel sick amount of treachery

Mix all of your ingredients together and you have the deliberate destruction of decades of life-saving work, irrevocable broken trust, and soft power diminished to zero. Additional seasonings include 10,000+ careers shattered, feelings of hopelessness and rage that are unimaginable.

My stomach dropped. My heart sank. My hope was shaken. I knew we could handle budget cuts. We'd managed them before, creatively, strategically, without losing sight of our core mission. But this wasn't about reducing programs or consolidating offices.

This was about something unprecedented.

When the Impossible Becomes Inevitable

USAID, the agency I'd called home for over 15 years, the platform I'd dreamed of leading, the mission field where I'd planned to serve communities across Rwanda and Burundi, was being dismantled.

Not reformed. Not restructured. Completely and utterly dismantled.

They instilled fear at the onset, like a bunch of cowardly bullies. It was like a scene out of the movies. On January 27th, they cut off the head, placing over 60 senior executives across the agency on administrative leave. That is when chaos took form. Then they started spewing lies, funding condoms in Gaza, which was actually an HIV/AIDS project in Gaza, Mozambique. While they told lies, they simultaneously took out our systems... websites removed, publications deleted... anything that could dispute what they said vanished. Then they attacked us, public servants, dedicated, committed to the greater good, and called us criminals and that we worked for a criminal organization. At one point these spineless souls demanded that we leave the countries we were serving in 30 days or they would remove us by force. The speed at which this happened was unbelievable. A congressionally mandated Agency for 65+ years, taken down in less than 3 months.

And the devastation to the nation of all of this? Honey, no one did a single thing about it. Not Congress, not the courts, NO ONE. We were alone on an island screaming for help and the world watched as we vanished into thin air. Well, the Agency that is, but the people, well we are built strong! Here's the thing about bullies, their victories are short-sighted and short lived and there is one thing that will await those treacherous without cause, SHAME!

The work we did wasn't just programs on paper. It was people. Real people whose lives depended on the partnerships we'd spent years building.

And the devastation wasn't limited to USAID employees. Partners around the world saw funding stopped haphazardly while they claimed they were reviewing the "efficiency" of programs. When the funding stopped abruptly, children died... literally. And when some of us tried to speak this truth, they claimed we were exaggerating. But the reality is, it was true, and no one did anything about it. The "Shock and Awe" worked like a charm.

Just like that, bullies with a recipe for disaster ate us for breakfast.

The Weight of Leadership in Crisis

What do you do when things aren't in your control? You control what is within your circle of influence. My first instinct was protection. Not of myself, but of my teams. In Rwanda and Burundi, I was leading people who'd dedicated their careers to this work, who'd trusted that their service mattered, who'd built their lives around the stability and purpose that USAID provided.

How do you tell someone that their life's work is being eliminated? How do you maintain morale when the very foundation of your mission is crumbling? How do you continue to lead when you don't know what you're leading toward?

I thought about Ambassador Lenhardt's words: "Take care of your people and they will take care of you." But how do you take care of people when their livelihoods have been taken from them?

The servant leadership principles I'd learned and practiced suddenly felt more crucial than ever. My team didn't need a leader who had all the answers, none of us had answers to something this unprecedented. They needed a leader who would stand with them, fight for them, and refuse to abandon them even when the institution was abandoning us all.

The Plan That Wasn't

As more details emerged, the magnitude of the failure became clear. This wasn't a carefully orchestrated transition with thought-out timelines and clear next steps. This was organizational chaos masquerading as policy reform.

There was no plan. And as every leader knows, a goal without a plan is just a dream. But this wasn't even a dream, it was a nightmare of institutional incompetence played out on a global stage with real human consequences.

They only gave us 5 months to shut down operations. Not just shut down operations, but plan our whole lives, take children out of school, relocate, find a home, find a job, find a sense of purpose. Find our next plan. There was no guidance on employee transitions. No coherent strategy for maintaining critical programs during the shutdown. No consideration of how partner governments would react to the sudden withdrawal of long-term commitments. The only thing that was planned was chaos... deliberate, devastating chaos.

I began to understand what my original draft had captured so viscerally: "This non-plan, this catastrophic failure of leadership and vision, was poorly executed, poorly implemented, poorly designed. It was, simply and tragically, poor in every way that matters."

Fighting for What's Right Begins

Standing in my office, looking out of my window, feeling a deep sense of sadness. Thinking to myself, I was supposed to be building lasting partnerships, the kind that take decades to cultivate and represent America's greatest strength on the global stage.

Soft power. That's what USAID represented. For over 65 years, USAID had been a bipartisan agency, created and sustained by both Democrats and Republicans who understood that America's strength wasn't just military might or economic coercion, but the power of partnership, trust, and shared values.

It's what made countries choose to work with us rather than against us. It's what turned adversaries into allies and skeptics into partners. It's the credibility that came from showing up, year after year, investing in people's futures, caring about communities beyond our borders, regardless of which party was in power.

And they were destroying it. Deliberately. Carelessly. Erasing sixty-five years of carefully built relationships with a stroke of policy ignorance. The partnerships I was supposed to be building. They were watching us abandon commitments mid-stream, break promises to vulnerable populations and prove that our partnerships meant nothing when political winds shifted.

Soft power isn't abstract. It's the reason governments trusted us with their most sensitive development challenges. It's why communities welcomed our programs. It's why partners believed in our long-term commitment. And in five months, they were burning it all to the ground.

But I made a choice that would define everything that came after: Fight. Fight even when no one else is fighting. Just fight.

My dad used to say, "if you don't stand for something, you will fall for anything." I wasn't going to let this chaos destroy my people without a fight.

I had no idea what this fight would look like. I didn't know it would mean sleepless nights crying, writing legal briefs that would be ignored. I didn't know it would require navigating settlement negotiations for my team while my authority was stripped from me for no logical reason. I didn't know that I would be facing my own financial devastation. I especially didn't know my own team would question my efforts when I was sacrificing everything for them.

All I knew was that servant leadership doesn't get to choose its battles. When your people need you most, when the institution fails them completely, when everything you were supposed to build is being torn down, that's when you discover what you're really made of.

The giants were falling. America's soft power was being dismantled by people who didn't understand what it was or why it mattered. But the servants? We were just getting started.

The question haunted me in those early days: Was I really unapologetic about taking care of my team? Would I step up when stepping up meant standing in the fire?

I was about to find out.

Part II: Standing in the Fire

Chapter 3: The Non-Plan

"There was no plan. And as every leader knows, a goal without a plan is just a dream. But this wasn't even a dream, it was a nightmare of institutional incompetence played out on a global stage with real human consequences."

Do you know what institutional violence looks like? It's not dramatic. It's not cinematic. It's bureaucratic incompetence masquerading as competence, leaving thousands of people to figure out how to rebuild their lives while the architects of destruction walk away unscathed. That's the hardest thing about this whole mess. It feels like the bullies are winning. How could they be sleeping at night? Knowing the harm they were causing to millions around the world. The morbid part is, these heartless people are sleeping very well, while tears soaked the pillows of people without hope.

There simply was no plan other than to destroy. The timeline for this destruction was rapid and bulldozed anyone in the way. The chaos and damage was intentional and aggressive and a complete abandonment of responsibility for the human wreckage they were creating.

Tick Tock

They gave us five months. On March 28th, reduction in force notifications were sent to all USAID employees, with various end dates. Mine was September 2nd. Five months to shut down operations that had taken decades to build. Five months to transition out of countries where we'd spent years building trust with governments and communities. Five months to pack up our lives, find new jobs, relocate our families, and somehow maintain our dignity while they told the world we were criminals.

Five months. I couldn't process 5 months. How do we do this in 5 months? Why 5 months? What was the rush?

Do you know what it takes to properly close a USAID mission? I had to do it for 2. The responsible transfer of programs, the careful transition of partnerships, the respectful coordination with host governments who had depended on these relationships for years? The thoughtful placement of staff who had given their careers to this work?

Years... It takes years.

But they didn't care about responsible transitions. They didn't care about our families, our children and quite frankly they didn't give a damn about us. They cared about spectacle, about the appearance of decisive action, about satisfying whatever political appetite or bruised ego that had demanded this destruction in the first place.

The Impossible Logistics

And what about our personal lives, my husband's career, which was tied to USAID? My children, the most innocent in all of this. How do I explain the unthinkable, or explain what you yourself don't understand? I remember reading a comment online about the dismantling of USAID, and someone said, "Welcome to the real world, people lose jobs all the time, get over it." As ignorant and as heartless as that comment was, it stung like a thousand bee stings. The reality is I had 5 months, and I had no idea where we were going, we had no home to return to in the States. Our lives, for the last 15 years, have been overseas.

So, what does five months actually mean for families serving overseas? Picture this:

You wake up one day and learn that not only are you losing your job, but you have to evacuate your life from a foreign country by a date that's already circled in red on someone else's calendar. Your children have to be pulled out of schools. Your spouse has to abandon whatever work or community involvement they'd built. You have to sell your belongings, find temporary housing, book international flights for your entire family, and most importantly pray you have enough savings to help you weather the storm. There is a sense of shame when you didn't plan for the unexpected. A sense of judgement from friends and family when they say, "how did you not have X amount of savings." And while you grin and bear their judgement, you then begin judging yourself.

And you have to do all of this while continuing to work, but not just work, lead, because the programs still need to be managed responsibly even as they're being destroyed, and your team needs you now more than ever. They are looking to you for next steps, EVERYONE is looking to you for next steps.

Just months before, I had raised my hand and sworn an oath: "I, Keisha Effiom, affirm that I will support and defend the Constitution of the United States against all enemies, foreign and domestic; that I will bear true faith and allegiance to the same; that I take this obligation freely, without any mental reservation or purpose of evasion; and that I will well and faithfully discharge the duties of the office on which I am about to enter."

I had taken that oath seriously. I believed in those words. And now the very government I'd sworn to serve was dismantling the agency through which I served, giving me five months to dismantle my life while still faithfully discharging my duties.

Oh, and you need to find a new job. Preferably before the five months are up, because your health insurance is going to be cut off, your severance package is delayed and your retirement benefits are delayed indefinitely. This non-plan didn't take into account that thousands of us will be leaving or retiring at the same time, leaving no one to process our paperwork. Suddenly, that shame you felt about your own non-plan becomes a hard reality.

But it's just a job, right? Just get over it, right?

The Human Resources Nightmare

Here's what makes it even more obscene: they knew they were creating an HR crisis of unprecedented proportions, and they did nothing to prepare for it.

Thousands of employees suddenly needing retirement processing. Thousands more needing severance calculations.

International relocations for hundreds of families. Health insurance continuations. Reimbursements for relocation expenses that people had already incurred during mandated repatriations.

You know how many additional HR staff they brought on to handle this tsunami of administrative need? Initially 4 additional staff, then a few more, but never enough to handle this monstrosity.

They actually made it worse by placing senior executives on administrative leave, eliminating the very people who understood how these complex processes worked. It was like performing surgery by first cutting off the surgeon's hands.

The Partner Betrayal

But the cruelest aspect of the non-plan wasn't what it did to USAID employees, it was what it did to our partners.

Imagine you're running a health clinic in a remote area, depending on USAID funding to provide HIV treatment to your community. You've spent years building this program, training staff, earning the trust of patients who are literally depending on you for their lives.

One day, with no warning, the funding stops. Not because the program isn't working. Not because the need has disappeared. But because someone in Washington decided that development assistance is inefficient and needs to be "reviewed."

Your patients still need their medication. Their lives still depend on the continuity of care you've been providing. But the review process? That could take months. Or longer. Who knows?

What do you tell the mother whose child depends on the nutrition program that just disappeared overnight? What do you tell the farmers who were in the middle of a growing season, depending on agricultural support that evaporated without explanation?

You tell them the truth: the people who made these decisions never bothered to think about you at all.

And you watch people, children... die. Despite what was said, people in communities died, children died and even some of our own colleagues took their own lives. PEOPLE DIED, and no one is talking about it and no one is acknowledging it. They are sleeping well at night, unbothered that death is on their hands.

The Diplomatic Disaster

From a foreign policy perspective, the non-plan was a masterclass in how to destroy decades of soft power in record time.

Governments who had built their development strategies around long-term USAID commitments suddenly found themselves abandoned mid-project. Bilateral agreements became worthless paper overnight. Countries that had trusted America as a reliable partner learned that our word meant nothing if the political winds shifted.

The damage to America's credibility wasn't just about USAID, it was about what it signaled to the world about how we treat our commitments, our partners, and our own people.

How do you explain to the government of Rwanda, which had worked closely with us on everything from health systems to economic development, that we were just... leaving? Not because they had done anything wrong, not because the programs weren't successful, but because of some internal political calculation that they had no part in making.

You can't. Because there's no explanation that doesn't sound like betrayal.

The Legal Violations in Progress

While all this chaos was unfolding, those of us who understood federal employment law could see the train wreck coming from miles away.

Foreign Service Officers separated under a Reduction in Force have specific legal protections. There are mandatory timelines for retirement processing. There are requirements for health insurance continuation. There are regulations governing how severance must be calculated and paid.

None of this was being followed. Not because they didn't know the law, but because they didn't care about following it.

I started documenting everything. Every missed deadline, every violated procedure, every failure to provide the basic protections that federal employees are guaranteed under law. Not because I thought anyone would listen, but because someone needed to create a record of what was being done to us.

That documentation would eventually become the legal brief I sent to headquarters, the one that would be ignored completely, but that colleagues around the world would request copies of because they needed someone to articulate what they were experiencing.

The Cascade of Incompetence

The worst part about watching the non-plan unfold was seeing how each failure created ten more failures down the line.

Because they didn't plan for HR capacity, retirement processing got delayed, which meant people couldn't access their earned benefits. Because health insurance transitions weren't properly managed, families lost coverage. Because there was no systematic approach to program transitions, critical initiatives collapsed, leaving beneficiaries stranded.

Every single one of these failures was predictable. Every single one could have been prevented with proper planning. Every single one created unnecessary human suffering that could have been avoided if the people making these decisions had cared about competent execution instead of political theater.

But competent execution requires admitting that the people you're destroying actually knew what they were doing. It requires acknowledging that the work being eliminated actually mattered. It requires treating career professionals as human beings rather than obstacles to your political agenda.

And they were constitutionally incapable of any of that.

Standing in the Wreckage

As the scope of the non-plan became clear, I realized that my role as a leader had fundamentally changed. I wasn't managing programs anymore; I was trying to protect people from institutional violence. I wasn't building partnerships; I was trying to preserve whatever dignity and support I could for my team while everything collapsed around us.

The servant leadership principles that had guided my entire career suddenly took on new meaning. When institutions fail their people this completely, servant leaders don't get the luxury of following normal procedures. We have to create new ways to take care of people, new methods of fighting for what's right, new strategies for preserving human dignity in the face of systematic cruelty.

I thought about words I had heard my whole life, from both my parents: "If you don't stand for something, you will fall for anything." Standing in the wreckage of the non-plan, I knew exactly what I was going to stand for.

My people. My principles. My FAITH. And the belief that nothing justifies destroying thousands of lives without a plan for what comes next.

The fight was about to begin in earnest. And I was ready for war.

Chapter 4: Fighting for What's Right

"Servant leaders don't get to choose comfortable fights. We fight for what's right, especially when it's inconvenient."

The information came during one of our daily briefings with what was left of leadership in Washington. My legal authority as Mission Director for Rwanda and Burundi was being removed and transferred to the State Department.

Let me be clear: just the authorities they didn't like.

What do I mean by that? Well, when it was time to put together compensation packages for my team, there were a couple of things that were required by law. One was to follow the local compensation plan for severance packages. But to avoid possible litigation with the USG, and let's be honest, none of this was legal and the possibility of litigation was real, Mission Directors, in consultation with our lawyers, local lawyers, and our executive officers, can also execute mutual settlement agreements (MSAs) with local employees.

I didn't hesitate, I wanted to give my team the best that we could, within the realms of the law. It was not a requirement to do MSAs. It was simply the right thing to do.

Full Steam Ahead, Until the Pushback

I was moving forward, full steam ahead, updating what was left of leadership in Washington during our daily calls and our embassy leadership. What was evident was that not every mission was pursuing MSAs. Some countries' local compensation plans were excellent, others weren't. So the need for an MSA varied. But those that were pursuing them found that some Mission Directors were getting pushback from their embassy leadership.

Why the pushback? Because State Department was about to go through their own RIF, and they weren't going to be offering their local employees anything more than what was legally required, severance packages in accordance with the local compensation plan. So some thought it wasn't "fair," or that USAID wasn't, "One team, One mission," if we offered our people more than they did.

This just speaks to the long history and battle between USAID and State about who is the big brother almighty. The funny thing is, there shouldn't be competition amongst us, when we are all fighting for the greater good. The State Department does diplomacy, USAID does development. Sorry, I digress.

The reality was, although State Department was in fact going to go through its own RIF, ours was drastically, unequivocally different. Our ENTIRE agency was being shuttered, while theirs was remaining.

The Squeaky Wheel Destroys Everything

So, while various Mission Directors were facing pushback on moving forward with MSAs, they raised it to our headquarters. And eventually, the squeaky wheel caused harm for all of us, and State Department required MSAs to be vetted through them for final approval.

Oh, and I forgot one important fact: when I say vetted through them, that doesn't mean their own legal department. Their legal department didn't want to touch this with a six-foot pole.

Did I forget to mention that our local employees are actually personal service contractors, and they can absolutely sue the USG in the states, while State Department locally employed staff are employees and they can only pursue litigation for wrongful termination in the country in which they work? I mentioned this to our State Department colleagues, and this fell on deaf ears.

Fighting an Impossible System

What followed was the strangest negotiation of my career, if you can call it a negotiation when the other side refuses to acknowledge reality.

Policies already existed. Legal frameworks were already in place. Our own legal counsel had already weighed in. None of it mattered. People with small minds and cruel instincts simply ignored what was inconvenient. They rewrote the rules in real time to justify doing as little as possible for people who had given everything.

In one meeting, someone asked me: "Why do you want to give them everything?"

Them.

Not "your team." Not "these public servants." Not "the people who dedicated their careers to this mission." Just... them. As if my colleagues were an inconvenience to be disposed of. As if their decades of service meant nothing. As if basic dignity was an unreasonable ask.

I wanted to scream. Every single day, I wanted to scream.

How could people not understand what was right? Where was the basic human kindness? Were people so rooted in their own entitlement, so disconnected from consequence, that compassion never even occurred to them?

I never laughed at the absurdity. There was nothing funny about watching colleagues get physically ill from the stress. Nothing funny about the cancer diagnoses, the heart attacks, the bodies breaking down under the weight of institutional cruelty. I can name four people, friends I called family, who are no longer here. Four people who didn't survive what was done to us.

So no, I didn't find the irony amusing. I found it devastating.

When this transferred over to State for final approval, I had the support of my Ambassador, but some in the embassy were completely against it. My heart was racing, I suddenly got hot, my eyes could pierce their soul. "Give them everything?" I asked in disbelief, "This doesn't even scratch the surface. For the record, giving them what they're due is keeping their jobs. I am doing what is right. Why does it bother you so much?"

They couldn't answer. Here were people questioning whether those who were losing everything deserved even basic support during their transition.

It was a moment that crystallized everything wrong with how this entire process was being handled, people making decisions about other people's lives without ever having to live with the consequences themselves.

This upset me greatly. If I can be blunt: It pissed me off!

But here's what I learned: when you can't control the process, you can still influence the outcome. When you don't have formal authority, you can still exercise moral authority. When the institution fails your people, you can still be their advocate.

The irony wasn't lost on me: I was trying to protect a government that wasn't protecting me at all, a government that had turned its back on me and thousands of dedicated public servants. Here I was, fighting to shield them from litigation while they stripped away my authority, delayed my benefits, and treated my expertise like an inconvenience.

The Bureaucratic Warfare

The irony was thick: State Department, which prided itself on diplomatic expertise, was creating a diplomatic disaster with our host governments by suddenly abandoning long-term commitments. Meanwhile, they were so concerned about appearing "fair" to their own employees that they were willing to risk massive litigation exposure rather than acknowledge that different legal categories of workers require different treatment.

And through it all, I kept thinking: this is what happens when people who don't understand the work try to dismantle the work. They break things they don't even know exist, create problems they can't foresee, and leave others to clean up the mess.

The Context They Couldn't See

While I was fighting these settlement battles, while I was researching the law and negotiating with indifferent bureaucrats, while I was spending sleepless nights trying to figure out how to take care of my teams, I was also dealing with my own crisis.

My retirement benefits were going to be delayed and no one could tell me for how long. Some would say maybe 3 months or 6 months, but not one single person could give me a definitive answer. Here was the problem, the Agency typically processed 100 retirements a year, now they are processing 1300 in less than 6 months, with a bare-bones staff and no additional help coming in. I was fighting for months of support for my teams while facing uncertainty for my own family.

But that's not something you share when you're trying to maintain morale. That's not something you burden your people with when they're already overwhelmed by their own uncertainty.

Servant leadership means you carry the weight privately while projecting strength publicly. It means you fight hardest for others when you're struggling most yourself.

The Breakthrough and the Heartbreak

After weeks of negotiation, legal research, and careful relationship management, we reached an agreement. It wasn't perfect, but it was something. It would help people transition. It would provide some stability. It would demonstrate that someone in this whole mess still cared about doing right by the people who'd served faithfully.

But let me tell you what it took to get here.

I fought battles my team never saw. I sat in rooms with people who questioned why I wanted to do anything for "them," and I answered with professionalism when I wanted to flip the table. I defended the humanity of my team to people who saw them as an inconvenience. I swallowed my rage and kept fighting.

You've read about the sleepless nights. The colleagues we lost. The bodies breaking down. The tears. I won't repeat it here. But know this: by the time we got that approval, I had nothing left. I had poured everything into this fight.

So when we finally won, I felt a moment of satisfaction, the first I'd experienced in months. We'd fought an impossible fight against impossible odds and achieved something meaningful for 100+ people who needed it most.

Then came the heartbreak.

Some of my team went behind my back to the Ambassador. They questioned my motives. They wondered if I'd done enough, fought hard enough, cared enough. People I had sacrificed for didn't see the sacrifice.

What I didn't know was that the hardest part was still coming.

What I didn't know was that fighting for your people sometimes means they don't understand you're fighting for them.

What I didn't know was that even when you win, it can feel like losing when the people you've sacrificed for question whether you sacrificed enough.

Chapter 5: The Ambassador Meeting

"Betrayal and broken trust, by whom..."

Now that the MSAs were finally approved on July 10th, I could turn my attention to my family. I needed to take some leave to put the pieces together for us and prepare for our next steps.

So, I took ten days off and my family and I traveled back to DC. During the midst of this circus, we decided that we did not want to return to the US. We had no home in the US and the cost of living was too expensive and to be quite honest, we had to go somewhere we could afford and where our savings would give us a cushion for a few months.

It's hard for me to admit that I couldn't fathom coming back home, this place that raised this savvy DC girl, educated an authentic woman and launched me into this global impact leader on the continent. That's when it hit me: betrayal doesn't always have a face. Sometimes it's systemic. Sometimes it's the slow, sinking realization that the country you represented abroad can't, or simply won't, make space for you to return.

I had served. I had built. I had given my career, my expertise, my years to something I deeply believed in with USAID. And when the bureaucratic machinery shifted, when USAID closed, I was left economically and emotionally exposed, my husband and I suddenly jobless, facing a "home country" that had become unaffordable and unwelcoming in ways I couldn't have imagined.

But it was more than economics. It was the realization that I didn't belong there anymore. I didn't feel like it was a place where my family and I could feel safe.

I had a 14-year-old son who loves his hoodies and cornrows. A 12-year-old daughter who still looks at the world with hope and possibility. A husband naturalized by a country he once believed in.

I refused to experience the emotional cost of an "accident" because my son fit the description. I couldn't watch my daughter's hope being shattered by a reality I couldn't protect her from. Or my husband, a naturalized citizen, somehow becoming deportable in a country that no longer played by its own rules. I had no faith to give. No hope. Not in this place I once called home. DC wasn't home anymore. Not in any way that mattered.

We had to rethink what home truly means. Is it where you grew up? Or is home where you can rebuild? Where your people are? Where you feel safe and like you belong?

So we decided to move to South Africa. Here we would have a community. Several of us affected by the closure of USAID were relocating to SA. Specifically, my sistah friends, Janean, Ana, Jackie, and Brianne. Besides my older sister, these are my ride or dies and we were all casualties of the same institutional failure. We were all impacted by this. We needed each other.

South Africa became home not because of roots, but because that's where the safety net existed. That's where belonging lived. That's where we could land together and catch our breath.

Home, I learned, is where you choose to make it when the place that made you no longer has room for who you've become.

So off to DC we went to apply for our retirement visa for South Africa. Those ten days were supposed to be about us, about figuring out how we were going to move to South Africa and stay overseas, about getting our documentation in order, about finally focusing on our own transition after months of putting everyone else first.

I thought my team understood. With only five months to dismantle our entire lives, I'd spent every waking moment fighting for my team's settlements, navigating bureaucratic obstacles, and trying to be their north star through the chaos. But I also had a family to think about, a future to plan, a life to rebuild after this institutional destruction. I needed a moment to take care of my family's future too.

I was wrong.

The Call That Changed Everything

The phone rang while I was at the South African consulate, about to enter the room for our visa interview. It was a colleague from the embassy, and their tone immediately told me something was very wrong.

"Keisha, I thought you should know. Your team called a meeting with the Ambassador. They're meeting with him right now to discuss the settlement outcomes."

The words hit me like a physical blow. My team, the people I'd been fighting for day and night, the people I'd been transparent with, the people I'd sacrificed my own peace of mind to keep informed, had gone around me to complain to the Ambassador about outcomes we'd fought to achieve for them.

While I was on leave. While I wasn't there to explain the context, to defend the process, to provide the perspective that only I had as the person who'd lived through every negotiation, every legal obstacle, every bureaucratic battle that had led to these settlements.

The Betrayal That Cut Deepest

Recipe for Betrayal by loved ones

- 1 tablespoon of selective memory
- A generous helping of ingratitude
- 1 cup of inability to see past their own pain
- A dash of impatience
- 2 cups of broken trust
- 1 pound of timing that cuts like a knife
- An unlimited amount of "I did this for your own good" justification
- Pour in until it hurts: the weight of being misunderstood by people you protected

Mix together and sit until betrayal forms.

The betrayal was made so much worse by the timing. I had finally, FINALLY, taken ten days to focus on my own family's future after months of putting everyone else first. For the first time since this nightmare began, I was trying to secure our own transition, to think about our own survival in a system that had given us just five months to rebuild our entire lives.

And this was when they chose to go around me.

It wasn't just that they'd gone to the Ambassador. It was that they'd done it the moment I stepped away to handle my own crisis. Without giving me a chance to address their concerns first. Without acknowledging that I might have explanations for the outcomes they were questioning. Without recognizing that as their leader, and as someone facing the exact same upheaval they were, I deserved the courtesy of hearing their grievances before they took them over my head.

The cruelest irony was that I was in DC doing exactly what they were upset about having to do, trying to figure out how to rebuild a life that had been destroyed by circumstances beyond my control. I was applying for visas, researching housing, planning a future in a foreign country, all while still carrying the emotional weight of their disappointments and my own uncertain future.

They couldn't wait ten days. Ten days for me to handle my own family's needs after months of prioritizing theirs.

The taxation issue that had them so upset, as if I had somehow chosen for their settlements to be taxed by the Rwandan government. As if I had the power to exempt them from local tax law. As if I hadn't explored every possible avenue to minimize their tax burden, only to run into legal requirements that no one could change.

They felt that promises had been broken, but the only promises that had been broken were the ones made by the system itself, the promise of fair treatment, adequate planning, and competent leadership from the people who'd created this disaster in the first place.

The Isolation of Leadership

Sitting there, processing what had happened, I felt more alone than I'd ever felt in my career. The people I'd been protecting, advocating for, fighting alongside had decided I was the enemy. The transparency that was supposed to build trust had somehow convinced them that I wasn't doing enough for them.

I thought about all the sleepless nights I'd spent researching legal precedents, crafting arguments, negotiating with indifferent bureaucrats who saw my team as nothing more than an administrative inconvenience. I thought about the personal costs I was absorbing, my own delayed benefits, my own uncertain future, while fighting for their stability.

I thought about the meetings where I'd been told to give them less, and how I'd pushed back. The conversations where officials questioned why I wanted to "give them everything," and how I'd defended their right to dignity and support.

None of that mattered now. What mattered was that they were disappointed with the outcomes, and in their disappointment, they'd decided that I was the appropriate target for their frustration.

The Ambassador's Position

I can't blame the Ambassador for taking the meeting. When staff request to speak with leadership about their concerns, good leaders listen. He was a good leader, a good man. I couldn't wrap my head around the need to do this while I was away, it felt like they went around me to present their case as if I were an obstacle to their wellbeing rather than their advocate. It revealed how badly I'd failed to help them understand the impossible circumstances we were all navigating.

Or maybe it revealed something else: that no matter how transparent you are, no matter how hard you fight, no matter how much you sacrifice, people in pain sometimes need someone to blame. And the person fighting hardest for them becomes the most convenient target.

When Self-Doubt becomes the Loudest Voice

I kept asking myself: Had I failed them somehow? Had my transparency created unrealistic expectations that made the final outcomes feel like betrayals? Had I not fought hard enough, not pushed back strongly enough, not found the right arguments to get them everything they deserved?

Had I failed them?

Absolutely not. This was my team. I loved them and I wanted to get them the best. I wanted them to have their jobs, the ones they poured their passion into. I wanted them to be made whole. But that wasn't possible, no one could give them that. What I could give them, what I fought day and night to secure, was dignity in transition, support beyond legal requirements, time to rebuild what had been taken from them. Did I fail them? No. But I couldn't save them from the pain of loss, and some confused that inability with unwillingness.

Or had I simply learned the hardest lesson of leadership: that sometimes the people you're trying to protect will turn on you when the protection you can provide isn't enough to shield them from all the pain they're experiencing?

Yes. That was the truth I didn't want to accept but couldn't deny.

The Deeper Heartbreak

What broke my heart wasn't just the meeting itself, it was what it represented. After everything we'd been through together, after all the battles fought on their behalf, they didn't trust me enough to bring their concerns to me first.

They'd decided that going around me was more likely to get them results than working with me. They'd concluded that I was part of the problem rather than part of the solution.

In their pain and disappointment, they'd forgotten that I was experiencing my own version of everything they were going through, and that I was fighting not just for their futures, but while facing complete uncertainty about my own.

The Weight of Ungrateful Hearts

This wasn't about needing gratitude or recognition for the work I'd done. This was about the fundamental breakdown of trust between a leader and the people she'd been fighting for. This was about realizing that servant leadership doesn't guarantee that the people you serve will understand what you're sacrificing for them.

The hardest part was knowing that if they'd come to me first, I could have explained the constraints I'd been operating under. I could have walked them through the legal obstacles, the bureaucratic resistance, the impossible choices that had shaped every outcome.

I could have helped them understand that every decision had been made with their best interests in mind, even when those decisions produced results that felt inadequate or unfair.

But they'd chosen to bypass that conversation entirely. They'd decided that my perspective wasn't worth hearing before they escalated their concerns to the highest level available to them.

The Leadership Crisis

This meeting represented more than just a breakdown in communication, it was a crisis of leadership authority. How do you continue to lead people who've essentially declared that they don't trust your leadership? How do you maintain team cohesion when some team members have gone around you to challenge the outcomes of battles you fought on their behalf?

How do you recover from the knowledge that your own team sees you as an obstacle to their wellbeing rather than as their advocate?

The Storm That Was Coming

I knew this meeting was just the beginning. If they were willing to go to the Ambassador while I was on leave, what would they be willing to do when I returned? How would I face a team that had essentially voted no confidence in my leadership by bypassing me entirely?

The worst part was knowing that the hardest conversation was still coming, the confrontation. I had to talk to my team and address my concerns about this meeting. To tell them how I felt about this type of betrayal. The transparency that was supposed to build trust had somehow created suspicion. The fight that was supposed to help them had convinced some of them that I wasn't fighting hard enough.

This was servant leadership at its most painful: continuing to serve people who had decided you weren't serving them well enough.

Part III: The Heart Breaks Open

Chapter 6: Transparency to a Fault

"My team went on an emotional rollercoaster."

Can someone be transparent to a fault? Looking back on everything, I wonder if I was too transparent with my team in all of this.

Not because transparency is wrong; I still believe in it as a core leadership principle. But because I learned the hard way that keeping people informed about an inherently chaotic process means they experience every twist, every setback, every moment of hope and disappointment in real time.

When you're transparent about a situation that's constantly changing, your team doesn't just hear the final outcome. They live through every negotiation, every reversed decision, every moment when what seemed certain becomes uncertain again.

And that can break people's spirits in ways that protect them from nothing and at the same time, prepare them for nothing. In an impossible situation like this, when your whole situation is based on lies from the delusional, you want to be that North Star for your team, so I had to be transparent, that's what they deserved — clarity amongst the fog.

My approach came from everything I'd learned about servant leadership. I believe people deserve to know what's happening, especially when it affects their livelihoods. Transparency can deflate anxiety, rumor-mongering, and a sense of powerlessness.

So I committed to keeping my teams informed throughout the settlement negotiations. When I had promising news, I shared it. When I hit obstacles, I explained them. When circumstances changed, I updated everyone immediately.

I thought I was treating my people with respect and dignity. I thought I was giving them clarity in a situation where they had very little control.

I thought transparency was always the right choice, until it's not.

What I didn't anticipate was how exhausting it would be for my teams to experience every emotional high and low of a negotiation process that stretched over months.

First, there was hope: Get the maximum we can, legally for our people. Then complexity: taxes, labor laws, contractor vs. employee. Then setbacks: loss of authority as mission director to make the final decision. Others getting involved that have no authority to make the decision. Then inequality: different package for Rwanda and a different package for Burundi. Equity was at the core of my decision making... when I had the authority to do so. I wanted everyone to get the same thing. So, for every update, there was a change, every change was a high on the roller coaster or a low on the roller coaster. Each update was factual. Each communication was honest. Each change was explained as thoroughly as I could manage given the constraints I was operating under.

But the cumulative effect was that my teams experienced weeks of uncertainty, hope, disappointment, and confusion, not because I was being dishonest or secretive, but because I was being transparent about an inherently messy and unpredictable process.

The facts: People started making decisions based on preliminary information that later changed. They built expectations around early proposals that had to be revised. They shared good news with their families that had to be walked back when circumstances shifted. Every changed decision required another changed solution.

Each change felt like a broken promise, even though I'd been careful never to promise anything that wasn't finalized. Each revision felt like a setback, even when we were actually making progress toward a resolution.

The transparency I thought would empower my teams ended up creating its own kind of suffering, the suffering of hope repeatedly raised and diminished, of expectations formed and reformed and formed again. To put it simply, it was EXHAUSTING — emotionally, physically, and mentally.

I started to realize that when you're leading during a crisis, your words carry weight that goes far beyond their literal meaning. When I said, "we're exploring options," people heard "we're going to get this option." When I said, "there are complications," people heard "things are falling apart."

Every update I gave was filtered through the anxiety, fear, and hope of people whose entire futures hung in the balance. The clinical language of negotiations became personal promises in their minds. The careful qualifications I added to every statement got lost in the emotional urgency of people desperate for certainty in an uncertain time.

I was trying to be honest about a terrible situation, transparent about a process designed to be opaque and quite honestly a process doomed to fail, straightforward about circumstances that were anything but straightforward.

And my team was paying the emotional price for my commitment to keeping them informed. I was paying the emotional price of leading with integrity, despite dishonest and cruel people.

The breaking point came during one of our regular team meetings. I was explaining the latest developments, another change in the settlement structure, another delay in the timeline, another complication that would affect the final outcomes.

I could see it in their faces: exhaustion, disappointment, and for some... maybe distrust. Not just from the uncertainty of their situations, but from the emotional labor of processing changes about situations they, nor I, couldn't control.

One team member pulled me aside and said: "Can you just tell us when it's final? These constant changes are harder to deal with than not knowing would be."

It was a moment that challenged everything I believed about leadership and communication. Was my commitment to transparency making things worse for the people I was trying to help? It certainly felt like it. And to be completely honest, the statement was fair.

I found myself in an impossible position. If I stopped providing updates, people would feel shut out of decisions affecting their lives.

If I continued providing updates about a chaotic process, people would continue experiencing that chaos secondhand.

If I only shared final decisions, people would feel like mushrooms, kept in the dark and fed bullcrap. If I shared the entire negotiation process, people would experience every setback as a personal disappointment. They had enough on their plates to deal with and remember I am supposed to be their north star amid this chaos.

There was no good answer. Every choice involved trade-offs between transparency and peace of mind, between respect and protection, between treating people as adults and shielding them from emotional turmoil they couldn't influence.

What made it worse was my own emotional investment in keeping my teams informed. Every update I gave came from a deep place of caring, every change I had to communicate felt like a personal failure, every disappointment they experienced became my disappointment too.

I was absorbing not just the stress of negotiating impossible settlements under impossible circumstances, but the emotional weight of my teams' reactions to information I felt obligated to share.

The servant leadership principle of transparency was creating its own kind of suffering, for them and for me.

The Lessons That Came Too Late

Looking back, I understand that there might have been a middle path. Maybe I could have communicated about the process without specific details about outcomes until they were finalized. Or just provided information about timelines without promises about results. Transparency about the challenges we were facing without creating false hope about solutions we might achieve. I believe all these things are true and here's what I also understand: we only had 5 months to wrap up this catastrophic nightmare. Every twist and turn, every emotional rollercoaster, every single setback was created by individuals who wanted to break us. Who wanted us to give up and do nothing. Who wanted us to be cowards that they were and I simply couldn't give them that satisfaction.

So, I defaulted to the humane and most respectful approach: tell people the truth about what was happening, when it was happening, as it was happening.

The Trust That Survived

Despite the emotional roller coaster, despite the constant changes, despite the exhaustion of processing uncertainty in real time, most of my team understood what I was trying to do. They recognized that the chaos they were experiencing through my updates was a reflection of the actual chaos of the situation, not a failure of my leadership.

They could see that I was fighting for them, even when the fights were messy and the outcomes were imperfect. They felt my tears and pain with every disappointing news received. They could tell that every change I communicated came from a place of respect for their right to know what was happening to their lives.

But some couldn't see past their own pain to understand the impossible circumstances I was navigating. And when the final settlements were announced, some of those team members would question not just the outcomes, but the efforts that had produced them.

That questioning would become the greatest test of my leadership during this entire crisis for a team I loved dearly and fought for unwaveringly. This was one of my greatest sources of heartbreak in a process that had already broken my heart in ways I didn't know was even possible.

The Wisdom That Remains

So, can you be transparent to a fault? Absolutely! But here's what I also know now: A dear friend told me that clarity and transparency are kindness. Kindness was needed during this tumultuous time. I wanted people to know what was happening and not to be amongst the fog, especially when it directly affected them and their families. You have to be transparent, even if you can't control the emotions that come with it.

Yes, my transparency created an emotional roller coaster. Yes, it may have contributed to unrealistic expectations. Yes, it made the journey harder for everyone involved.

But what was the alternative, keeping my team in the dark while their lives fell apart around them? That would have been a betrayal to them and of everything I believed about servant leadership. They deserved to know. They deserved clarity amongst the chaos. They deserved kindness, even when that kindness came with difficult truths and changing circumstances.

Would I do it differently? Maybe I'd find better ways to manage expectations while maintaining honesty. But would I abandon transparency? Never. Because even when transparency is painful, even when it creates problems, even when it leads to betrayal, it's still an act of respect for people's right to know what's happening to their own lives.

Chapter 7: The Confrontation

"Transparency doesn't always build trust"

The time had come to confront my team. I stared at the connect button on my screen. Racing thoughts in my head... as I sat there staring at the screen I thought about what that meeting with the Ambassador should've been. It should have brought clarity, but instead it brought blame. Blame of me on the unfavorable changes, a team questioning my honesty and I couldn't believe it. Here is what is critically important to understand about Rwandans and their trust: once you break it, you never get it back. I knew the devastating effects of not being honest and I was not willing to break that. So, to think that some felt like I wasn't being honest... was crushing. When I heard that, I was ANGRY! Do they know how hard I fought for them, what hoops I had to jump through, what faces I wanted to slap, the amount of cold-hearted, insensitive, heartless conversations had with people that didn't give a damn about them or a darn settlement agreement because it didn't affect them. Every day felt like a 12-round fight. One day I'd get my ear bitten off like Holyfield. The next, a sting from Ali I never saw coming. Some days I was on the ropes, wondering why I ever stepped in the ring. I had to keep getting up, bruised, black-eyed and all.

But when we got the call from Washington on July 10th that it was finally approved, I cried. Not the silent cry, the fall down to your knees, can't catch your breath cry. I looked up to the sky and thanked Jehovah for getting us across the finish line.

Days later, I was standing in the South African Embassy in D.C., fighting for my family's retirement visas while my own benefits sat in limbo. The embassy was chaos. Rude staff, incompetent processes, a diplomatic relationship fraying at the edges. No one was giving us answers about our future.

And then I learned: some of my team was questioning whether I'd been honest with them.

I felt the betrayal hit my chest before my brain could process it. My first thought wasn't gracious. It was raw: I have been fighting for you while my own life falls apart, and you question me?

I wanted to quit. Just... stop.

But I didn't. Because advocating for them was the one thing I could still control. And to have that integrity questioned, even by one person, broke something I'm not sure I've fully repaired.

I couldn't wrap my head around this, so I had to have this call with them. I had to confront them or else I would never get to say my piece. So, I took a deep breath, prayed for guidance and clicked connect.

Here's the irony, I was calling into a meeting from my own desperate situation to address their complaints about outcomes I'd fought to achieve for them. And once again, I had to put my situation on the back burner.

When the meeting started and I saw their initials in those little video boxes, I could feel the tension in my shoulders and chest immediately. Everyone's cameras were off, except for mine. I wanted them to see my face. I didn't want to come across as angry, but I was, I didn't want to come across as hurt, but I was. The truth is, I could only be authentically me and I was angry and I was hurt. In order for me to lead in this moment, despite my hurt and anger, I had to remind myself of my own words, "give myself and others grace, lead from a place of good intentions and boldly know that what I did was grounded in truth and justice for them". I knew I had to remind them that the world crashing around us is not our own doing. I took another deep breath and said, "I want to talk about the meeting held with the Ambassador while I was on leave."

The silence was deafening, even on Zoom.

"I'm disappointed," I said, "Not in the settlements we achieved, those represent victories against impossible odds. I'm disappointed by some of the things said in that meeting."

I paused, trying to keep my voice steady, trying to maintain my professionalism while my heart was breaking.

I knew I needed to simply state the facts, what I did, how we got here and where we went from here. I talked about gratitude. I told them that perspectives matter when you're making decisions about trust and leadership.

I took a breath and dove into the deep water.

"While you were upset about taxation on your settlements, my own retirement benefits are delayed indefinitely. While you were concerned about the amounts you were receiving, some aren't receiving anything, a situation you were almost in. While you were frustrated with the timeline, several of us don't have a timeline, we have been left with, we don't know when you will receive your annuity, or other's health insurance ends in thirty days."

Another deep breath, to give myself space to hold it together.

"I wasn't sharing this with you before because it wasn't your burden to carry. I was supposed to be your north star, your source of stability. But when you went to the Ambassador to question the outcomes many of us fought so hard to achieve while facing my own devastating circumstances, perspective became important."

"Do you know what we had to do to get these settlements?" I asked, and now my voice was getting stronger, fueled by months of suppressed frustration. "Do you know about the meetings where officials asked me why I wanted to 'give you everything'? "Do you know about the nights spent crafting arguments to justify settlements that went beyond legal requirements? Do you know about the bureaucrats who didn't want to approve anything for you because it would make their own employees jealous?"

The silence stretched on.

"We fought people who saw you as an administrative inconvenience." These are the unknown battles that were being fought.

"And while I was doing all of that," I continued, "I was also dealing with the fact that my own benefits were being delayed, my own future was uncertain, my own family was facing upheaval that was just as dramatic as what you were experiencing."

One team member finally spoke up: "We didn't know,"

"You didn't know because I didn't burden you with it," I interrupted. "Because my job was to be your advocate and your stability, not to add my problems to your stress. But when it was perceived that promises were broken or perhaps, I wasn't fighting hard enough for you, perspective and facts became relevant."

This was the hardest part, but it had to be said.

"You felt that promises had been broken, but the only promises that were broken were the ones made by the system that created this disaster in the first place. I never promised you specific amounts or specific timelines, I promised to fight for you. And I did. Every single day."

"So now you have a choice, you can focus on what the settlements don't include, or you can recognize that they represent support beyond what was legally required, achieved against impossible odds by someone who was facing her own version of everything you're going through and I want to be extremely clear, I will not explain myself again on this matter."

I left the call, feeling emotionally drained. I thought to myself, "they can see me as the leader who didn't get them everything they wanted, or they can see me as the leader who fought battles they couldn't see to get them more than the system ever wanted to give them.

As I thought about that call in the evening, I felt like I'd lost something that could never be recovered: the innocence of believing that fighting for people guaranteed they would understand what you were fighting against.

Some team members approached me afterward with apologies and expressions of gratitude. But the damage to our relationship, to my faith in transparent leadership, to my belief that servant leadership would be recognized and appreciated... that damage felt permanent.

I learned that you can't please everyone. I had learned that transparency doesn't always build trust. I had learned that fighting hardest for people sometimes makes you the target of their frustration when the fight doesn't produce perfect results.

Most painfully, I had learned that even servant leaders sometimes have to serve people hard truths about gratitude, perspective, and the real cost of the battles being fought on their behalf.

My heart was broken. But the work had to continue. The mission had to go on. And somehow, I had to find a way to keep leading people who had taught me that love and loyalty don't always run in both directions.

That team meeting changed me forever. It was the moment I realized that servant leadership sometimes means serving people consequences for their choices, even when, especially when it breaks your heart to do it.

Chapter 8: Learning You Can't Please Everyone

"The loneliest leadership lesson."

In the days following the call with my team, I found myself replaying every decision I'd made, every communication I'd shared, every battle I'd fought. Was there something I could have done differently? Some way I could have managed the process that would have prevented this breakdown of trust?

I was learning the hardest lesson of leadership: No matter how much you care, no matter how hard you fight, no matter how much you sacrifice, you can't please everyone. And sometimes, the people you fight hardest for will be the ones who are least satisfied with what you achieve.

This lesson reshaped everything I thought I knew about servant leadership.

After months of fighting for settlements that went beyond legal requirements, after securing outcomes that many missions couldn't achieve for their teams, after absorbing personal costs while advocating for their stability, I was faced with a reality I'd never anticipated: some people would focus entirely on what they didn't receive rather than acknowledging what had been achieved against impossible odds.

The mathematics were simple but painful. Even if 80% of your team understands what you've accomplished, the 20% who don't will consume your thoughts, drain your energy, and make you question everything about your approach to leadership.

That 20% becomes 100% of your sleepless nights.

I realized I'd fallen into a trap that catches many servant leaders: believing that if you care enough, work hard enough, and communicate transparently enough, everyone will eventually understand and appreciate your efforts.

But leadership isn't a mathematical equation where good intentions plus hard work always equals gratitude and understanding. Leadership is messier than that, more unpredictable, more human.

To be fair, people process disappointment differently. People have different expectations, different ways of measuring success, different capacities for seeing beyond their own immediate concerns to understand the broader context of what's happening around them.

And some people, no matter what you do for them, will never be satisfied with anything less than everything they wanted, delivered exactly the way they wanted it, regardless of circumstances beyond anyone's control.

One of my deepest assumptions about servant leadership had been that loyalty would be reciprocal. If you fight for people, they'll understand you're fighting for them. If you absorb costs on their behalf, they'll recognize the sacrifice. If you put their needs before your own, they'll appreciate the priority you've given them.

But loyalty isn't always reciprocal. Trust isn't always mutual. And understanding doesn't always follow explanation, no matter how thorough or transparent that explanation might be.

Some people will interpret your transparency as lies rather than honesty. Some will see your explanations of constraints as excuses rather than context. Some will focus on the gap between what they wanted and what they received rather than the distance between what they received and what they almost lost.

There's a particular loneliness that comes with being misunderstood by people you've been trying to protect. It's different from being criticized by opponents or strangers, that you can dismiss or defend against. But when the people you've been fighting for decide you weren't fighting hard enough, when the people you've been transparent with decide you've been dishonest, when the people you've sacrificed for question your motives, that is damaging.

That kind of misunderstanding makes you question not just your decisions, but your entire approach to leadership. It makes you wonder if caring is weakness, if transparency is naivety, if fighting for people just sets them up to be disappointed when you can't deliver everything they want.

In those moments after the confrontation call, I understood why some leaders become distant, transactional, focused on outcomes rather than relationships. Why they stop sharing information that might create expectations. Why they protect themselves by caring less, engaging less, investing less of their hearts in the people they lead.

It would be so much easier to lead with emotional distance. To make decisions without consulting people who might disagree with them. To announce outcomes without explaining the process that led to them. To focus on what's legally required rather than fighting for what people deserve.

But that would mean abandoning everything I believed about servant leadership. It would mean letting the 20% who couldn't see beyond their disappointment change how I served the 80% who could.

The lesson wasn't that I should stop caring or stop fighting for people. The lesson was that I needed to care and fight without expecting universal understanding or appreciation in return.

I needed to learn to measure success not by whether everyone was satisfied, but by whether I'd done everything I could within the constraints I was given. Not by whether everyone appreciated my efforts, but by whether those efforts had achieved meaningful results for people who needed them.

I needed to accept that some people would always focus on what was missing rather than what was present, what went wrong rather than what went right, what they didn't receive rather than what they almost lost.

This experience forced me to redefine what success looked like in servant leadership. Success wasn't universal satisfaction, that was impossible in a crisis where no outcome could fully compensate for the losses people were experiencing.

Success was knowing that I'd fought every battle I could fight, absorbed every cost I could absorb, and achieved every outcome that was possible within the constraints of an impossible system.

Success was knowing that most of my team understood what had been accomplished on their behalf, even if some couldn't see past their own disappointment to recognize it.

Success was maintaining my integrity and values even when those values weren't universally appreciated or understood.

I learned that servant leadership has limits, not in how much you're willing to give or fight or sacrifice, but in how much you can control other people's responses to your service.

You can fight battles they can't see, but you can't make them understand the battles were fought.

You can absorb costs on their behalf, but you can't make them appreciate the costs you absorbed.

You can achieve outcomes that seemed impossible, but you can't make them focus on what was achieved rather than what wasn't.

Those limitations don't diminish the value of servant leadership, they just make it more realistic about what servant leaders can and can't accomplish.

The Peace That Comes With Truth

There was something liberating about accepting that I couldn't please everyone. It freed me from the impossible burden of trying to manage every person's emotional response to circumstances that were beyond anyone's complete control.

It allowed me to focus on doing what was right rather than what would be universally popular. It let me make decisions based on what was possible rather than what would satisfy every individual preference.

Most importantly, it taught me that servant leadership isn't about being universally loved or appreciated. It's about serving people's actual needs, even when they don't recognize those needs being met, even when they focus on what you couldn't provide rather than what you did.

The Leadership That Survives

The leaders who survive crises like this aren't the ones who please everyone, those leaders don't exist. The leaders who survive are the ones who can absorb disappointment, misunderstanding, and even betrayal while continuing to serve the people who need them most.

They're the leaders who can say "I did everything I could within the constraints I was given" and mean it, regardless of whether everyone appreciates what "everything" looked like in practice.

They're the leaders who understand that you can't control outcomes, only efforts. You can't control other people's responses, only your own integrity.

And sometimes, that has to be enough.

The Lesson That Changes Everything

Learning that you can't please everyone isn't just a leadership lesson, it's a life lesson that changes how you approach every relationship, every decision, every effort to help other people.

It teaches you to find satisfaction in doing right rather than being appreciated for doing right. It helps you focus on the people who can see and understand your efforts rather than those who can't or won't.

Most importantly, it frees you to keep caring, keep fighting, keep serving, not because everyone will appreciate it, but because it's who you are and what the world needs, regardless of universal appreciation.

The loneliest leadership lesson became the most liberating one: I couldn't please everyone, and that was okay. My job wasn't to be universally loved. My job was to fight for what was right, take care of the people I could help, and maintain my integrity regardless of how those efforts were received.

Some people would understand. Some wouldn't. Both groups deserved my best efforts, even if only one group would recognize them.

Chapter 9: "We Aren't Going to Cry"

"Recognition amidst the ruins."

The US Embassy Kigali Awards Ceremony. I sat next to my deputy, we had been through it, standing in the fire. We were bruised, exhausted and mentally drained. This work, a place we called home, was scattering into pieces. Our livelihoods of 20+ years were being ripped away from us and we were leading a 100+ person team through this upheaval. We sat in this awards ceremony wondering what exactly we were celebrating and trying to maintain the composure expected of senior leaders at formal events. The ceremony was winding down, various awards had been presented, and I was mentally preparing to return to the endless tasks of managing mission closure while supporting a heartbroken team.

Then the Ambassador stood up to present one final award.

"This year," the Ambassador began, "we are creating a new recognition. The first-ever US Embassy Kigali Leadership Award."

My deputy and I exchanged a glance.

The Award No One Expected

"This award," the Ambassador continued, "recognizes sustained superior performance leading the USAID Mission Rwanda team through unprecedented reforms while delivering greater safety, security and prosperity for the Rwandan and American people."

I would later read the official certificate: "US Embassy Kigali Leadership Award presented to Keisha Effiom, for Keisha Effiom's sustained superior performance leading the USAID Mission Rwanda team through unprecedented reforms while delivering greater safety, security, and prosperity for the Rwandan and American people."

Every word of that citation would come to mean something to me. "Sustained superior performance" — not just surviving, but excelling. "Unprecedented reforms," the diplomatic language for institutional destruction. "Greater safety, security, and prosperity," we'd maintained our mission even as the institution crumbled.

The room went quiet. Everyone knew what "unprecedented reforms" meant. Everyone understood that "leading through" was a euphemism for surviving institutional destruction.

I leaned over to my deputy and whispered, "We aren't going to cry."

She nodded. "We aren't going to cry."

We were both lying.

The Recognition That Broke Us

As the Ambassador described the leadership that had been demonstrated during the crisis, the battles fought, the people protected, the partnerships maintained even as the institution crumbled, I felt something crack open inside me that I'd been holding closed for months.

This was the first time anyone in a position of authority had publicly acknowledged what we'd been through. The first time someone had said out loud that what we'd done was difficult, meaningful, was worthy of recognition.

Not just tolerated. Not just accepted. Recognized. Honored. Valued.

The Ambassador called our names. My deputy and I stood, and that's when the tears started. Not the silent, professional tears you can blink away. The kind of tears that come from a place so deep you didn't know it existed until something touches it.

The Standing Ovation

We walked to the front of the room, and the entire embassy stood up. Not polite applause while remaining seated. A full standing ovation, with cheers and tears shed by others who saw our fight, who felt our love, who saw us. They'd watched what we'd been going through. They'd seen us show up every day, trying to maintain professionalism while everything fell apart. They'd witnessed the impossible balancing act of closing missions while caring for devastated teams. They witnessed two black women, forged together in unity, fighting for a team they loved sincerely and deeply. Caring for each other, protecting each other and showing this mission real leadership. No egos, no pride. We led with love, faith and justice. We did what was right, even when others didn't want to. We simply led. Their applause and recognition seemed to go on forever.

My deputy and I stood there together, holding each other's hand, openly crying, and receiving recognition we hadn't asked for, hadn't expected, but in some way, desperately needing it in ways we hadn't fully understood until it was offered.

What the Award Represented

This wasn't just recognition of our administrative competence or our ability to manage complex operations. This was acknowledgment of something deeper, that we'd maintained our humanity, our integrity, our commitment to servant leadership even when the institution we served was being destroyed.

We'd kept showing up for our teams when we could have checked out emotionally. We'd fought battles we could have avoided. We'd absorbed costs we could have deflected onto others. We'd maintained standards of excellence when mediocrity would have been completely understandable given the circumstances.

And someone had noticed. Someone had seen. Someone had decided that leadership in crisis deserved recognition, not just sympathy.

The Validation We Didn't Know We Needed

For months, I'd been questioning everything about my leadership approach. Had I failed my team? Had my transparency created problems? Had I fought hard enough? Was I doing enough?

And here was an external authority, someone who'd watched the entire process from a different vantage point, saying clearly and publicly: what you did was extraordinary. What you achieved was remarkable. How you led was worthy of the first award of its kind.

It didn't erase the betrayal I'd experienced from some team members. It didn't solve the problems we were still facing. It didn't change the reality that USAID was still being dismantled and lives were still being upended.

But it provided something I'd been missing: external validation that my efforts had been seen, understood, and valued by people whose judgment I respected.

The Moment That Changed Everything

Standing there with my deputy, both of us crying while the embassy applauded, I realized something important: I'd been so focused on whether my team appreciated my leadership that I'd forgotten that leadership isn't measured by universal approval within your immediate circle.

Leadership is also measured by whether you maintained your integrity under impossible circumstances. Whether you fought for what was right even when the fight was lonely. Whether you served people even when they couldn't see the service being rendered.

The Ambassador wasn't recognizing us for pleasing everyone. He was recognizing us for doing what needed to be done, the way it needed to be done, regardless of whether it was universally appreciated.

The Speech I Couldn't Give

I should have given a speech. That's what you do when you receive awards. You say something gracious and inspiring and appropriate to the moment.

But I couldn't speak. My deputy couldn't speak. We just stood there, crying, trying to absorb the magnitude of being seen and valued after months of feeling unseen and unappreciated.

Eventually, we managed to thank the Ambassador and the embassy team. We said something about the honor of serving and the privilege of leading during difficult times. But the words felt inadequate to capture what that moment meant.

Sometimes recognition hits you in places you didn't know were wounded. Sometimes validation reaches depths you didn't know existed. Sometimes being seen is so powerful that words become unnecessary.

What My Deputy and I Shared

My deputy and I had walked this journey together. She'd experienced her own version of every battle I'd fought, absorbed her own costs, faced her own disappointments. We'd supported each other through the darkest moments, picked each other up when one of us was ready to break, shared the burden of leadership when it felt too heavy for one person to carry.

Receiving this award together meant everything. It wasn't just individual recognition, it was acknowledgment that we'd survived this together, that servant leadership doesn't have to be a solitary journey, that having someone who understands in your corner makes impossible situations survivable.

We weren't going to cry. But we did cry. Together. In front of everyone. And somehow, that felt like exactly the right response. She will forever be my sister for life, my ride and thrive, my sistah friend. I couldn't have gotten through this without her.

The Paradox of Recognition

The paradox was that we were being honored for leadership during the destruction of the very institution we'd dedicated our careers to serving. We were receiving awards while managing the closure of missions we'd poured our hearts into building. We were being celebrated while our teams were preparing to leave work they loved.

It was recognition amidst the ruins. Validation while everything fell apart. An acknowledgment of excellence in the midst of institutional failure.

But maybe that's exactly when recognition matters most. Not when everything is going well and success is easy to measure. But when you're in the trenches, when the institution is failing, when you're questioning whether anything you're doing matters, that's when someone saying "we see you, we value you, what you're doing is extraordinary" can literally save you.

The Perspective It Provided

This award gave me perspective I desperately needed. I'd been so consumed by the team members who questioned my leadership that I'd lost sight of the broader picture, that most people could see what I was accomplishing, that external observers understood the impossible circumstances I was navigating, that my leadership was visible and valuable to people beyond my immediate team.

It reminded me that servant leadership isn't measured by universal approval from the people you serve. It's measured by whether you maintained your principles, fought for what was right, and served with integrity regardless of how those efforts were received.

Some team members would never understand or appreciate what I'd done for them. But others saw clearly. And people watching from outside my immediate circle could see even more clearly because they had perspective I couldn't access while I was in the middle of the fight.

The Gift of Being Seen

The greatest gift of that ceremony wasn't the award itself, though the first-ever US Embassy Kigali Leadership Award meant more than I could adequately express. The greatest gift was being seen.

After months of feeling invisible, misunderstood, unappreciated, to have someone stand up and say publicly "we see what you're doing, we understand how hard it is, and we recognize it as exemplary leadership" was oxygen to someone who'd been holding her breath for too long.

We weren't going to cry. But we needed to cry. We needed to release months of held tension, suppressed emotion, accumulated grief about everything that had been lost.

And somehow, crying while being honored felt like exactly the right way to process it all. The tears weren't weakness, they were acknowledgment of how hard we'd been fighting, how much we'd been carrying, how deeply we'd been affected by everything we'd been through.

The Memory That Sustains

When I think back on the entire USAID closure experience, that moment, standing with my deputy, crying while the embassy stood and applauded, will always stand out as the moment that made everything else survivable.

Not because it fixed anything. Not because it changed the fundamental reality we were facing. But because it reminded me that good leadership doesn't go unnoticed, even when it feels invisible. That fighting for what's right matters, even when the people you're fighting for can't see the battles being fought. That maintaining integrity and humanity in impossible circumstances is worth doing, regardless of universal appreciation.

We weren't going to cry. But we did. And in crying while being honored, we found a kind of healing we didn't know we needed.

The giants had fallen. The institution was being destroyed. Our teams were being scattered. Our own futures were uncertain.

But in that moment, we were seen. We were valued. We were recognized for maintaining excellence in the midst of catastrophe.

And somehow, that made all the difference.

Part IV: What Remains

Chapter 10: Seeds Scattered

"We are scattered, yes, but like seeds."

I stared at my computer screen for a long time before I started typing. This would be my last official communication to the teams I'd fought so hard for. What do you say when you yourself don't believe in goodbyes? How do you honor something that should never have ended?

I thought about everything we'd been through together, the Marburg response that deepened our value, the settlement battles that tested my leadership, the transparency that created both connection and complications, and the recognition that reminded me why I fought.

And I realized the message needed to be about what endures when institutions fail. About what we carry forward when everything else is taken away. About hope in the face of devastation. Hope was the foundation of how we survived this brutal attack, not the fragile kind that depends on circumstances, but the steady kind that is anchored in faith.

Here's the thing about hope: it's not naïve, it's sacred. Hope is the quiet conviction that God is still at work, even when everything looks lost. It's the belief that purpose outlives position, that bonds outlast bureaucracy, and that light does not need permission to shine again. Hope does not rest in what is seen, but in what is unseen, the promises still unfolding, the grace still at work, the future only God can see.

Now, the alternative to hope is something far more dangerous. When we lose hope, we make room for cynicism, and cynicism corrodes from the inside out. It steals clarity, compassion, and courage, three things a leader can never afford to lose. If I had allowed bitterness to take root, I would have led from my wounds instead of my wisdom. And that's not leadership; that's surrendering.

So even as I close this chapter, I do so with gratitude and expectancy. Because the same God who walked us through this fire will also lead us into new beginnings. The work continues, in different forms, through familiar and unfamiliar hands, and most importantly the work continues because we know the importance and nothing can ever stop it. And that is enough.

With Gratitude and Hope - Thank You and Until next time

August 4th, 2025. The final message.

Dear Team,

As we approach August 9, I find myself reflecting not only on the incredible work we've accomplished, but on the extraordinary people I've had the honor to work alongside.

Serving with each of you, in Rwanda and Burundi, has been one of the great privileges of my career. You have shown resilience in the toughest times, unending brilliance, and unwavering dedication in times of growth, challenge, and now, in the face of USAID's unexpected closure. Some of you have dedicated over two decades to this mission, becoming pillars of impact, wisdom, and hope for your communities and this institution.

While we didn't get to choose this ending, we do get to carry forward the legacy we built together. The lives we've touched, the systems we've strengthened, and the futures we've helped shape, none of that can be undone. These accomplishments live on, as do the bonds we formed.

To my colleagues, teammates, and friends: thank you. Thank you for your integrity, your laughter, your endurance, and your belief in something bigger than any one of us. You have been more than co-workers; you've been family.

As you all know, I know this is not the end. We are scattered, yes, but like seeds. We are planted everywhere now, taking root in new soil, carrying with us the values, purpose, and light that defined our time at USAID. People will remember the tremendous work we have done in Rwanda and Burundi, and around the world. And I will always remember each and every one of you.

These words by the late John Lewis, really helped us through this tumultuous time and I want us to carry this with us as we begin our new chapters with our heads held high: "We will not get lost in a sea of despair. We will not become bitter or hostile. We will remain hopeful and optimistic. Never, ever afraid to make some noise and get into some good trouble. We will always find a way to make a way out of no way."

See you soon. It has truly been an honor!

*With deep love, sincere gratitude and profound admiration,**
*Keisha

The Subject Line That Said Everything

"With Gratitude and Hope - Thank You and Until next time." I'd agonized over that subject line. Others might have written "Farewell" or "Final Message" or "Goodbye." But I couldn't. Even facing institutional destruction, I needed them to know this wasn't an ending, it was a transformation.

"Until next time" was a promise. I knew we would meet again, in different contexts, under different circumstances, but carrying the same commitment to service that had brought us together in the first place.

The Moment of Sending

At 10:01 AM East Africa Time on August 4, 2025, I hit send. The morning felt right, a new day, even in the end. The email went to 100+ people across two countries, multiple time zones, and countless life circumstances. FSNs facing unemployment, American officers being recalled, partners losing decade-long relationships, communities losing support systems.

10:01 AM. Just after the start of the workday, when people were settling in with their coffee, checking their inboxes, perhaps still believing in the possibility of reversal, of last-minute salvation. One minute past ten o'clock, somehow that single minute past the hour felt significant, like stepping just beyond a threshold into something irreversible.

I watched the email leave my outbox and felt something shift. This wasn't just professional correspondence, it was a covenant. By refusing to say goodbye, by insisting "see you soon," by invoking seeds and light and John Lewis's defiant hope, I was making a promise that USAID's closure couldn't break the bonds we'd formed.

Within minutes, the responses started coming. I knew not everyone would respond, some were too hurt, too exhausted, too focused on survival. But those who did reminded me why every battle had been worth fighting.

The Words I Almost Didn't Include

I hesitated over "you've been family." After the betrayal, after the Ambassador meeting, after the devastating confrontation, was that still true? Could I honestly say that people who'd questioned my honesty and gone around me to complain about outcomes I'd fought to achieve were family?

But I realized that family doesn't mean perfect. Family doesn't mean everyone always understands or appreciates what you do for them. Family means you keep showing up, keep caring, keep fighting for them even when they hurt you.

They were family. Even the ones who'd broken my heart. Especially the ones who'd broken my heart. Because that's what family does, they hurt you in ways others can't, precisely because they matter more than others do.

The Seeds Metaphor

"We are scattered, yes, but like seeds." This image had been sustaining me through the final months of closure. We weren't being destroyed, we were being dispersed. The institution was gone, but the people who'd made it meaningful were going everywhere, seeds scattered by institutional destruction taking root in new places. Some would land in other development organizations. Some would find private sector opportunities where they could apply their expertise differently. Some would return to their home countries and build something new from scratch.

But wherever they landed, they'd carry USAID's legacy with them. The skills we'd honed together. The values we'd lived by. The commitment to serving others that had brought us to this work in the first place.

The John Lewis Quote

I'd been holding onto John Lewis's words like a lifeline during the darkest moments: "We will not get lost in a sea of despair. We will not become bitter or hostile."

It would have been so easy to become bitter. So justifiable to become hostile. The betrayal by our government, by some colleagues, by the system itself gave us every reason to despair, to harden, to lose faith and hope in the possibility of doing meaningful work in broken institutions.

But John Lewis understood something essential: bitterness and hostility don't hurt the people who wronged you, they poison your own ability to move forward. Despair doesn't punish those who caused your pain, it robs you of hope for what comes next.

"We will remain hopeful and optimistic. Never, ever afraid to make some noise and get into some good trouble."

This was the legacy I wanted for my team. Not despair, but hope. Not bitterness, but the courage to keep fighting for what's right in whatever context they found themselves next. Not hostility, but the willingness to make good trouble when necessary.

The Responses That Healed

After I sent that final message, the responses started coming in and they reminded me why I'd fought so hard for them.

"Thank you for your beautiful and heartfelt words. Your leadership has been a constant source of inspiration... It is an honor to have worked alongside you, and I will carry the lessons of your leadership with me always.", Josephine*

"Under your leadership, we have grown, not just professionally, but also in confidence and purpose. You mentored, encouraged, and equipped us with the tools to climb to the next step.", Chantal*

"Your tears were full of strength... What gave me strength in those difficult times was seeing how you carried your pain with grace and resilience.", Mama Zoe*

"I am walking out of the Embassy compound with much confidence and pride.", A team member who'd found strength despite losing everything*

That last one broke me open in the best way. Despite everything, the institutional betrayal, the personal devastation, the uncertainty about their futures, they were walking out with confidence and pride. Not broken. Not defeated. Stronger, somehow, for having survived this together.

That's what servant leadership is supposed to accomplish. Not protecting people from all pain but equipping them to walk through pain with dignity intact.

The Burundi Team's Message

The message from the Burundi FSNs team arrived a few days later, and it destroyed whatever composure I'd managed to maintain:

"We recognize that the journey was anything but easy. Yet, through your persistence, resilience, and dedication, you not only carried the process forward but you also demonstrated the very essence of servant leadership. At a time when FSOs are still not receiving the recognition or distinction they deserve, your selfless efforts stood out all the more."

They saw it. They understood. While I'd been facing my own financial devastation and benefit delays, they'd been watching me fight for their settlement agreements. They'd recognized that I'd prioritized their stability over my own, their futures over my own comfort.

"We are aware that some of you may have already transitioned out of the USAID network. We kindly ask Keisha to help ensure this message reaches those who are no longer in the system."

Even in their own moment of loss, they were thinking about the others who'd fought for them. That's the legacy of servant leadership, it multiplies itself. People who've been served learn to serve others.

What We Carried Forward

As the final days approached and my team members began their transitions to whatever came next, I started to see what we were actually carrying forward. Not just technical skills or professional networks, but something deeper.

We carried forward the knowledge that institutions fail, but people endure. That leadership during crisis looks different from leadership during stability. That transparency has costs, but so does secrecy. That you can't please everyone, but you can maintain your integrity regardless.

We carried forward the understanding that serving others doesn't guarantee appreciation, but it guarantees you'll be able to look at yourself in the mirror. That fighting for what's right is worth doing even when you lose. That taking care of people matters even when they can't see the care being provided.

Most importantly, we carried forward the conviction that the work continues. The mission didn't end with USAID's dismantling, it simply evolved, expanded, became something bigger than any single institution could contain.

The Scattering That Was Actually Planting

In those final weeks, as I watched team members leave one by one, I started seeing the scattering differently. What had felt like destruction was actually dispersion. Seeds being carried by wind to places they could never have reached on their own.

My sistah friends and I, heading to South Africa together, creating a community of support and shared purpose in a new place. Team members finding opportunities in other development organizations, taking USAID's values and expertise to new institutional contexts. My team leveraging their skills and experience to build new careers in Rwanda and Burundi.

We'd been planted everywhere. And everywhere we landed, we'd grow something that reflected what we'd learned and who we'd become through serving together.

The giants had fallen. But the servants were already rising in new places, ready to serve in new ways, carrying forward the legacy of an institution that could be destroyed but whose values and impact would endure in the lives of everyone it had touched.

The Final Goodbye

On August 9, most of my team logged out for the last time, but for senior leaders like myself, we had one more duty - to be the last ones standing, to turn out the lights on an institution we'd served for decades.

For three more weeks, I walked through increasingly empty hallways where hundreds of USAID staff once rushed between meetings, debated strategies, and celebrated victories. Now, I was the only one left in the embassy. The silence was deafening.

On August 22, 2025, I carried out our USAID signage with my own hands, the physical weight of it couldn't compare to what it represented. Eighteen years of service, countless lives changed, systems strengthened, futures shaped. All of it reduced to a sign I could lift alone.

My vision blurred with tears as I walked through the embassy doors. The Marines, young men who'd watched us come and go for years, who'd seen our late nights and early mornings, our celebrations and now our devastation, they understood the moment. Without a word, they held the doors open, standing at attention as I carried our sign out for the first and last time.

It was a recognition that something significant was dying, something worth saluting even in its death. It signified a military honor for a civilian ending, a recognition that even those who guard our embassies understood: something irreplaceable was being lost.

As I placed the sign in the vehicle, I thought about everyone who'd already gone. But being the last one standing meant something too. Someone had to witness the final moment. Someone had to carry the sign. Someone had to receive the Marines' salute on behalf of everyone who'd served.

On September 2, I logged out of my USAID email for the last time. Eighteen years of service, countless battles fought, innumerable lives touched, all of it coming to an end because of decisions made by people who'd never understand what they'd destroyed.

But as I closed my laptop, I wasn't thinking about what had been lost. I was thinking about what I endured.

No one is saying that we did things perfectly, we never claimed perfection. We claimed conviction, that doing what was right would always matter more than doing what was easy. We claimed progress, integrity, and the unwavering belief that our work could still make a difference, even when the world said otherwise.

We were scattered. But we were also planted. And what grows from seeds scattered by destruction will be more resilient, more widespread, more impactful than anything that stayed safely in one place.

The work continues. It must continue. It will continue. Now we heal and grow.

Chapter 11: The Testament

"When giants fall, the servants remain."

I wrote these words, when giants fall, the servants remain, in June 2025, sitting at my dining room table in a place that my family and I called home for the past three years. My family and I had been diplomats, traveling around the world doing work that actually mattered, work that meant something. It was surreal that after 18 years of dedicated service, this was the ending. But was this the ending, or was this the beginning of something more powerful, more impactful, something unbreakable?

So much remained. They couldn't destroy everything.

What They Took

"They took my agency. The one I'd served for over two decades, the one where I'd risen from a Contracting Officer to one of only 8 African American women Mission Directors in the agency. The place where I'd learned that development work wasn't about being saviors, it was about partnership, about working yourself out of a job, about building capacity until you were no longer needed."*

"They took my home. Not the physical structure, but the spiritual home that USAID had been. The place where my calling aligned with my core values, where servant leadership wasn't just tolerated but celebrated, where "taking care of people" was strategy, not sentiment."*

"They took my platform. The position from which I could advocate for my team, fight for local staff who'd risked everything to work with us, champion development approaches that actually worked because they were rooted in respect, not charity."*

"They took our trust. They tried to treat us like criminals. Public servants working in places others wouldn't. They defamed our character and lied. They tried to break us and turn us against each other. They simply and boldly took... everything they could get their hands on."*

"They took our budgets and called it efficiency. They took our programs and called it streamlining. They took our partnerships, decades in the making, and called it reorganization."*

"They took soft power that generations had built and traded it for the hardness of indifference. They took our symbol of hands held to the world and formed it into a fist."*

"They took our tears, so many tears. In bathroom stalls, in empty offices, in cars after impossible meetings."*

"They took LIFE. Good people, strong people who simply couldn't manage this stress."*

"They took our health, our sleep, our peace. They took pieces of our hearts with every person we couldn't save, every promise we couldn't keep, every farewell we had to say."*

"They took the honor of service and made it feel like shame. They took the pride of representation and made it feel like abandonment. They took the calling of a lifetime and made it feel like failure."*

They were thorough. They were systematic. They were cruel in their completeness.

"Get Over It"

To everyone who says "get over it, people lose jobs every day," let me tell you what you don't know.

I was on a call with a State Department HR employee about our retirement packages. This person, whose job was to help us transition, told us we were "the worst bunch of people they had ever worked with." They disabled the chat and comments so they could be the only one to speak. Then they proceeded to insult every individual on the call, saying documents were incomplete, signatures were missing, forms were wrong. Never once acknowledging that we had five months to dismantle our entire lives. Never once acknowledging that their systems weren't built to process thousands of retirements at once. Never once acknowledging that maybe, just maybe, we were doing the best we could under impossible circumstances.

And here's the part that made my blood boil: this same person announced on the call that they were retiring. They hoped we would treat the next employee better. Let that sink in. They had the luxury to plan their retirement. They would walk off the job and receive their benefits immediately. Meanwhile, we're still waiting months later, and they had the audacity to lecture us about our frustration.

Then they told us that every time we contacted Congress about the delays, it pushed our cases further back. They were punishing us for advocating for ourselves. Punishing us for using the democratic process. Punishing us for refusing to be silent.

Some would say they weren't the ones who did this to us, so why take it out on them? But this person proved how heartless people can really be.

Heartless. Cruel. And completely unbothered.

Meanwhile, State Department employees who retired after us have been prioritized. They're receiving their payments. We're still waiting. Same government. Same system. Different treatment. The insult on top of the injury.

And it doesn't stop there.

The defamation of our character has followed us into the job market. Organizations have told former USAID employees to remove the Agency from their resumes. Job solicitations have explicitly prohibited hiring anyone with USAID experience. Let that sink in. Decades of public service, billions in development impact, lives saved and communities transformed, and we're being told to hide it like a criminal record.

They tried to permanently damage our lives. They tried to erase not just our Agency, but our ability to work, to provide for our families, to rebuild. And they did it without a care in the world.

So to the people who say "get over it," who roll their eyes at our grief, who think this is just about losing a job:

You have no idea what you're talking about.

This isn't about a job. This is about being labeled criminals by your own government. This is about watching colleagues die from the stress. This is about being told your decades of service make you unhireable. This is about a system that chewed us up, spit us out, and then blamed us for bleeding.

Get over it?

No. I will not get over it. I will speak on it. I will write about it. I will make sure the world knows what was done to us and who did it.

That's not bitterness. That's accountability.

And if that makes you uncomfortable, good. It should.

What They Couldn't Touch

But here's what I learned in those dark months, watching an institution die while trying to keep its people alive:

There are things that can't be dismantled by executive order, that can't be destroyed by vindictiveness, that can't be scattered by political winds. There are things they couldn't touch, no matter how hard they tried.

They couldn't take my calling. It was never about USAID. It was about service. About seeing a need and responding. About using whatever platform I had, whether Mission Director or private citizen, to make a difference where difference was needed.

They couldn't take my integrity. Every decision I made, I can defend. Every fight I fought was for others. Every tear I shed was honest. I said my piece, with peace, because peace doesn't come from institutional validation, it comes from knowing you stood when standing was costly.

They couldn't take the seeds. We are everywhere now. Scattered like seeds across the development landscape, taking root in new soil, preparing to bloom in ways they never imagined. The people at USAID and their families, they carry the DNA of real development work. They know what servant leadership looks like because they lived it, even when it was being destroyed around them.

They couldn't destroy the lessons. That mother in Burundi whose baby received the Plumpy'Nut peanut butter from USAID and said, "Now he will grow, "will always remember the impact of our work, because her child is alive. We cared, deeply. We loved, unconditionally, we served, fully.

The Servant Leader's Testament

So here is my testament, written through pain but not in defeat, not in triumph but in truth:

Servant leadership is about service itself, not about the institution you serve.

But first, let me give you the recipe, the real one. Not the recipe for destruction that created this disaster, but my heartfelt recipe for servant leadership that sustained me through it:

The Recipe for Servant Leadership

Ingredients:

- An unlimited supply of courage (you'll need more than you think)
- Immeasurable faith (in people, in purpose, in the possibility of change)
- An overflowing vessel of love (especially for those who don't love you back)
- A bottomless well of forgiveness (for others and yourself)
- Heaping portions of compassion (particularly when it's undeserved)
- Generous measures of understanding (even when you're misunderstood)
- Endless reserves of hope (store extra, you'll need it in the dark)
- Industrial strength will (the kind that bends but never breaks)
- Pure, undiluted integrity (no substitutions accepted)
- Abundant grace (apply liberally to all situations)
- Patient persistence (the slow-cooking kind)
- Righteous anger (just a pinch, but make it count)
- Sacred stubbornness (for refusing to abandon your people)
- Radical transparency (warning: this ingredient may sting)
- Humble strength (the kind that kneels to lift others up)

Instructions:

1. Begin with courage, you cannot serve without it
2. Mix in faith until you believe impossible things
3. Fold in love gently but thoroughly, it must touch everything

4. Add forgiveness daily (this ingredient expires quickly)
5. Layer compassion throughout, especially where it seems unwarranted
6. Blend understanding until smooth, removing all lumps of judgment
7. Let hope rise naturally, never punch it down
8. Strengthen with will, kneading until resilient
9. Bind everything with integrity, this holds it all together
10. Season generously with grace
11. Allow to rest in patience, then test with adversity
12. If mixture begins to harden, add more grace
13. When nearly complete, add righteous anger sparingly for backbone
14. Finish with sacred stubbornness, this preserves everything
15. Serve transparent and warm, with humble strength

Yield: Enough to sustain you through institutional collapse, personal betrayal, and professional devastation while still having plenty left over to share.

Storage: Keep in heart, refill daily through service. Never run out, the more you use, the more you have.

Warning: This recipe will transform you. Side effects include: sleepless nights fighting for others, tears in embassy conference rooms, standing ovations from those who see your truth, and an unshakeable peace that transcends circumstances.

Note: No substitutions. Attempts to replace integrity with expedience, courage with comfort, or love with indifference will cause complete failure. This recipe only works when all ingredients are genuine.

This is what I mixed every morning. This is what sustained me when the giants fell. This is what multiplied when we were scattered like seeds.

When they asked me to lead a mission with no plan for managing its closure, I created one. Not because headquarters deserved it, but because my people did.

When they denied us legal authority to help our staff, I fought for it anyway. Not because I thought I'd win, but because fighting for your people is what leaders do.

When they made me stand before 100+ people and explain why their lives were being destroyed by decisions I didn't make, I stood there. Not because I had answers, but because leaders don't run from hard moments.

When the Embassy gave my deputy and me their first-ever Leadership Award while everything was falling apart, we cried. Not because we were weak, but because being witnessed in your struggle is holy.

The Truth About Giants

The giants have fallen. The institution that was supposed to represent American generosity, partnership, and development excellence, it fell to ego, vindictiveness, and ignorance. It fell because small men needed to feel big, because complex problems got simple, cruel solutions, because expertise was treated as opposition.

But when giants fall, servants remain.

We remain in every clinic that still functions in Burundi. We remain in every Rwandan health worker who knows how to identify Marburg symptoms. We remain in every partnership that survived the institutional collapse. We remain in every local staff member who learned that real leadership looks like someone fighting for you even when the fight is hopeless.

The Final Truth

I started this journey with such hope. Standing in that conference room in DC, taking my oath, declaring "THE TIME IS NOW, MY TIME IS NOW, OUR TIME IS NOW!" I thought I was beginning a new chapter of building, creating, expanding impact.

Instead, I was called to practice servant leadership in its purest form: serving when the institution you serve is crumbling, leading when there's nowhere to lead people except through loss, fighting when victory means simply that your people's dignity remains intact even as everything else falls apart.

Would I do it again?

In a heartbeat.

Would I fight harder?

Every single day.

Because this is the testament of a servant leader: You serve not because institutions are worthy, but because people are. You lead not because you'll win, but because someone must stand in the gap. You fight not because victory is assured, but because surrender is unacceptable.

What Grows from Ruins

They thought they were ending something. They were really beginning it.

Every person who lived through this failure now knows what servant leadership actually looks like. They've seen it tested by betrayal, institutional and personal. They've watched it persist through impossible circumstances. They've witnessed it choose service over self-preservation, people over position, integrity over comfort.

These seeds, my scattered team, they don't just carry technical skills to their new positions. They carry the knowledge of what it looks like when someone fights for you against impossible odds. They carry the memory of leadership that says "we aren't going to cry" and then cries anyway because shared tears in struggle are sacred.

They carry the testament: That servant leadership isn't about the servant or the leadership. It's about the hyphen between them, that sacred space where calling meets crisis, where integrity meets impossible choices, where love for people transcends organizational charts.

My Name Is Keisha

My name is Keisha Lanai Effiom.

I am the daughter of parents who taught me that service is not optional.

I am the student of mentors who showed me that taking care of people is strategy.

I am the leader who stood in the rubble and declared the work continues.

I am the servant who learned that sometimes serving means being scattered like seed.

I am the woman who said her piece, with peace.

And I am not done.

The giants have fallen, but this servant remains. The institution is gone, but the mission endures. The platform has changed, but the calling is eternal.

This is not an ending. This is a testament. A witness. A declaration.

That what they meant for evil became preparation for something greater. That every seed scattered will grow. That every lesson learned in loss becomes foundation for what comes next.

The time is still now.

My time is still now.

Our time is still now.

And we are just getting started.

They asked me once what I would tell future leaders facing impossible circumstances, leading through institutional collapse, serving when service seems futile.

I would tell them this: Write your testament not in your victories but in your defeats. Let them see you cry when crying is honest. Fight battles you cannot win because your people deserve a champion. Say your piece, with peace, because peace doesn't come from outcomes, it comes from integrity.

And when they scatter you like seed, remember: Seeds grow wherever they land.

Especially seeds that have been tested by fire.

This book is my testament, but it's not my finale. It's my commencement. The beginning of whatever comes next.

To my scattered seeds still waiting for benefits: The delay is cruel, but it's not the end.

To those still grieving what we lost: Your grief honors what mattered.

To those building new things from the rubble: You are the future they tried to prevent.

To those who asked if I'd do it again: Look at us. We're doing it. Differently. Wiser. Scarred but still serving.

We're still standing. Still growing. Still healing. Still serving. Still here.

And this, this book, my testimony, my proof of survival, is just the beginning.

THE END OF THIS CHAPTER... THE BEGINNING OF EVERYTHING ELSE

Chapter 12: Blooming

"The Continuing Mission"

I'm writing this from a place of healing. Not victory, not triumph, but healing.

It's November 2025. Many of us are still waiting for our benefits to start. Still fighting for what was promised. Still navigating the aftermath of institutional violence. Still looking for jobs. The cruelty didn't end when USAID closed, it continues in every delayed payment, every ignored request, every reminder that to them, we were disposable.

And in spite of it all: We're blooming anyway.

The Seeds Take Root

My phone carries messages from the scattered:

"Still waiting on my retirement, but I started consulting. Using everything I learned."

"I got hired. It doesn't pay much, but it's a place to start."

"Some days are hard. Some days I'm angry. I'm focusing on healing so I can show up and be my best self."

"Found a position with the World Bank. They value what USAID taught us."

We're not all thriving. That would be a lie. Some of us are still wrestling with what happened. Still grieving. Still processing. But we're all still here. Still serving in whatever ways we can. Still refusing to let them win.

What Fighting Harder Really Looks Like

I thought fighting harder meant battling the system. Now I know it means building something new.

My sistah friends and I are starting a company. Launching in 2026. We're creating a place where servant leadership isn't just tolerated but celebrated, where taking care of people is the business model, not an afterthought. We get to show up and celebrate our authentic selves.

I'm working on a podcast. Not to relive the trauma, but to teach the lessons. To reach people who are standing in their own fires right now, wondering if they can survive. They can. We're proof.

This book you're reading? It's just the beginning. There are more stories to tell, more lessons to share, more servants to strengthen.

Fighting harder now means healing deliberately. Growing purposefully. Building intentionally.

The Peace That Transcends Understanding

People ask me how I can be at peace after everything that happened. How I can say I'd do it again when I'm still processing trauma, still watching colleagues struggle.

Here's the truth: Peace doesn't come from justice being served. It rarely is. Peace comes from knowing you served anyway.

Peace comes from the messages from my team: "It's hard, but I know we will be ok. Thank you for fighting for us."

Peace comes from knowing that every person I fought for knows someone fought for them.

Peace comes from understanding that they could take my position but not my purpose. I am still here, I am still me. Flawed, bruised and battle-tested.

I am at peace because I said my piece, with peace. Not in anger, though anger would be justified. Not in bitterness, though bitterness would be understandable. But with the deep, unshakeable peace of someone who knows she stood where she was supposed to stand.

The Next Version of Me

This isn't the version of me that took the oath in July 2024. That woman believed institutions could be saved. That good intentions could overcome bad systems. That if you just served hard enough, loved deep enough, fought long enough, you could change things from within.

This version of me knows better. And knows more.

This version knows that:

- Servant leadership doesn't require anyone's permission
- Healing is not a betrayal of the struggle
- Growing beyond trauma is the ultimate victory
- Peace is a choice, not a circumstance

This version of me is building outside the system that failed us. Creating alternatives. Nurturing options. Planting gardens in grounds they said were too damaged to grow anything.

The Truth About Starting Over

We're all wounded healers now. All carrying scars that look like wisdom. All determined to create what we needed when we needed it.

We're not trying to rebuild USAID. We're building something better. Something that can't be destroyed by ego or politics. Something that serves people, period.

This is what doing it all over again looks like: Not repeating the past, but learning from it. Not recreating what was, but creating what should be.

The Continuing Mission

Would I do it all over again? I am. Just differently.

Would I fight even harder? I am. Just smarter.

The mission that called me to USAID didn't die when USAID died. It transformed. It matured. It learned that institutions fail but missions endure. That giants fall but servants remain. That you can scatter seeds but you can't stop them from growing.

We are all becoming our next versions now. Some faster than others. Some with more struggle. But all of us carrying forward what matters: the knowledge that service isn't about where you serve but how. That leadership isn't about title but about showing up when showing up costs everything.

www.ingramcontent.com/pod-product-compliance
Ingram Content Group UK Ltd.
Pitfield, Milton Keynes, MK11 3LW, UK
UKHW041851190726
13854UKWH00002B/833